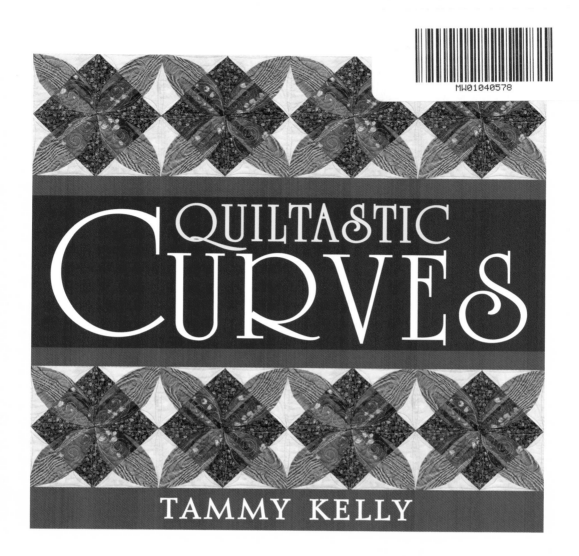

QUILTASTIC CURVES

TAMMY KELLY

Martingale®
& C O M P A N Y

Quiltastic Curves
© 2008 by Tammy Kelly

That Patchwork Place® is an imprint
of Martingale & Company®.

Martingale & Company
20205 144th Ave. NE
Woodinville, WA 98072-8478 USA
www.martingale-pub.com

Credits

President & CEO • Tom Wierzbicki
Publisher • Jane Hamada
Editorial Director • Mary V. Green
Managing Editor • Tina Cook
Technical Editor • Nancy Mahoney
Copy Editor • Melissa Bryan
Design Director • Stan Green
Production Manager • Regina Girard
Illustrator • Robin Strobel
Cover Designer • Stan Green
Text Designer • Regina Girard
Photographer • Brent Kane

Printed in China
13 12 11 10 09 08   8 7 6 5 4 3 2 1

Library of Congress Cataloging-in-Publication Data
Library of Congress Control Number: 2007045974

ISBN: 978-1-56477-783-6

Mission Statement
*Dedicated to providing quality products
and service to inspire creativity.*

Dedication

To Dave, my husband and best friend

Acknowledgments

My thanks go to the following:

The staff at Martingale & Company for their ongoing support

Sandy Muckenthaler for supplying me with batik fabrics from Hoffman Fabrics

Kathy Miller for supplying me with Fairy Frost fabrics from Michael Miller Fabrics

Odegaards Sewing Center, Quilter's Market, Quilter's Mercantile, Quilter's Store Sedona, and
Sun Valley Quilts for supporting local designers and willingly displaying my quilt samples

My very special friends who are always encouraging me in my creative ventures:
Brenda Whitted, Gay Aguirre-White, Heather Lady, Risa Dyer, Shannon Clifford, and Sue Lewis

Machine quilter Linda DeVries for her expertise and creativity with long-arm quilting

My daughter, Lynnae Kelly, who taught me to enjoy the color purple

My husband, Dave Kelly, who encourages me to do what I love

God continues to bless my work, and my hope is that it will be a blessing to others.
We can get very creative because we have the Spirit of the Creator living in us!

Contents

Introduction

Quilters today have become so sophisticated; I have found they are looking for a challenge in piecing and fabric selection. In this book, I've compiled 12 projects ranging in size and difficulty, specifically designed with the intermediate to advanced quilter in mind. With step-by-step directions and confidence-building suggestions, curved piecing will not be such a daunting task for those seeking new quiltmaking experiences.

Fabric-selection tips are provided for each project, and I encourage you to step out of your comfort zone. "Autumn Luster" on page 18 features warm browns and rusts, "Melon Patch" on page 50 uses just two colors, and "Quiltastic" on page 65 contrasts black with bright colors. Design sheets following each project will allow you to experiment with your own color choices. Many of the projects use small (⅛- to ¼-yard) pieces of multiple fabrics, which is a great way to use up your acquired stash and incorporate a variety of batiks.

Full-size template patterns are provided along with rotary-cutting suggestions for using acrylic templates. You may begin with a pattern that requires two templates and then progress to using four templates. You will learn how to play with the template patterns by cutting the designs in half, vertically or horizontally, to make an all-new design.

Detailed instructions and helpful illustrations are provided for sewing curved seams, which, in most instances, require only three pins. Sewing and pressing tips will assure accurate, quality blocks. Once you have read the section "Curved Piecing Techniques" on page 7, you will see just how easy it is to design, cut, and sew a quilt with curved lines.

In "Quiltmaking Basics" on page 11, I explain the methods I use, from cutting through quilt completion. As you become more experienced, you will find that there are many ways to complete the same task. I encourage you to try new techniques and use the methods that produce the most satisfying results.

I hope these projects will prove to be just the beginning as you become a confident curved piecer. Who knows? You may find that you can't go back to straight seam piecing after discovering the world of curves.

Curved Piecing Techniques

You may wonder where designers get their ideas. Being visual learners, we are constantly looking around and soaking up what we see, which later becomes part of our next creation. So after publishing my first two books, I was in a quandary. What next? My eyes fell on one of my antique quilts, most likely from the late 1800s. It had never been one of my favorite quilts, yet I had purchased it 15 years earlier at an antique store when I was decorating with an Americana theme. I laid it on the floor and quickly discovered that it was merely a combination of 6" blocks. I knew I wanted a contemporary look, so I chose batik fabrics and wow, what a difference they made in this early curved piecing design, which was historically named Love in a Tangle.

My first curved pieces were patterned after a well-worn paper template. Later I found that professionally laser-cut acrylic templates added to the accuracy and speed of my cutting techniques. So that's how my love of curved piecing was born. The effective use of color in "Mesmerize" on page 28 was such a success that I looked around to see what else I could try with curves. I had purchased a set of twin antique quilts made with the grandmother's-apron and housedress fabrics that were so popular in the 1930s. Upon doing a little research, I discovered that this Mohawk Trail quilt setting was just a variation of the common Drunkard's Path pattern. I was inspired to use updated frosted fabrics and continue with the scrappy theme as in the original quilt. As a result, "Bits of Shimmer" was born in varying shades of green and purple, as you can see on page 45. I tried to choose the least common Drunkard's Path variations when I developed "Stars 'n' Curves" on page 34 and "Splish Splash!" on page 40.

The antique quilt designs Love in a Tangle and Mohawk Trail provided creative inspiration.

Examining the Shapes

When designing quilts with curved piecing, consider the many different ways the template can be used to divide the fabric pieces.

 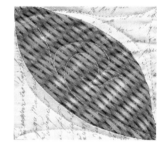

Combined with strategies for color placement, these multiple variations can aid you in developing the most creative designs. You can make photocopies of the line drawing following each quilt; then color the drawing using colored pencils to experiment with your own color choices. Once you have an understanding of how the pieces are put together and formed into blocks, you will feel more confident about approaching curved piecing.

The projects are listed in order from the easiest to the most challenging. The first 9 projects require only two templates each. Templates A, B, C, and D have a gentle curve that is easy to manipulate, much like sewing a sleeve in a garment. Templates E and F, used for "Melon Patch" on page 50, "Radiance" on page 55, and "Subtle Shades" on page 60, have a steeper curve, requiring more easing and sewing experience. "Scrap Blossoms" on page 72 uses three templates, and "Blazing Star" on page 78 uses four templates. These projects are geared for the intermediate to advanced quilter due to the steeper curves and complexity of the piecing.

Using Curved Templates

You can use acrylic templates, created specifically for the projects in this book, or you can make your own templates using the patterns that are included for each project. With either method you'll start by cutting strips in the width specified in the cutting instructions. Then follow the cutting directions for each project to make the best use of the fabric and note the appropriate grain line.

Curved acrylic templates are available from your local quilt store or by mail order from the author (see "Resources" on page 95). The ¼" acrylic templates will assist with cutting ease, speed, and accuracy and can be used with rotary cutters. To use an acrylic template, start by placing the fabric strips or pieces on a cutting mat. Then place one hand firmly on the template and use your other hand to cut around the template with a rotary cutter. I have found the OLFA Rotating Mat and a 28-mm rotary cutter to work particularly well when cutting curved templates. Cut around one curved edge, rotate the mat 180° without moving the fabric or template, and continue cutting around the remaining portion of the template. With the 28-mm rotary cutter, the small blade cuts easily around the curves without nicking the template. You can also cut accurately through several layers of fabric.

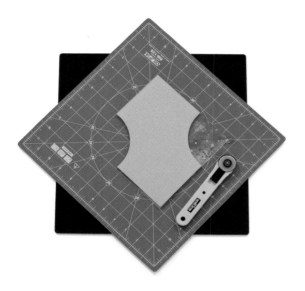

If you prefer, you can make your own templates by using a fine-point permanent pen and template plastic. Start by placing a piece of template plastic over the full-sized template pattern for the quilt you are making. Then, trace the lines of the shape onto the plastic. Mark the grain line and label the template. The seam allowances are already included, so you don't need to add them. Use utility scissors to carefully cut out the templates, cutting exactly on the drawn lines. Use a washable marking pen to trace the template shapes onto the fabric. You can use a rotary cutter and ruler to cut on the straight lines and then carefully cut out the curved areas of the fabric pieces with scissors.

Sewing Curves

The traditional Drunkard's Path pattern, which I incorporated into the quilts "Stars 'n' Curves," "Splish Splash!" and "Bits of Shimmer," can be used to demonstrate the steps involved in curved piecing. Looking at the two pieces in the Drunkard's Path unit, you can see that one has an inner curve, known as the concave curve, and the other piece has an outer curve, called the convex curve.

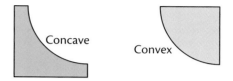

The template patterns include registration marks for matching one piece to another. These marks can be transferred onto the fabric pieces to help line up the pieces during piecing. However, I prefer a method that does not require marking. For example, with the Drunkard's Path unit I fold each piece in half and crease to mark the midpoint. Then I match up the creases and pin in place. I typically use three pins to hold the pieces together, one in the center and one at each end. You will find that all the patterns require a certain amount of easing to make them fit. I ease between the pins as needed.

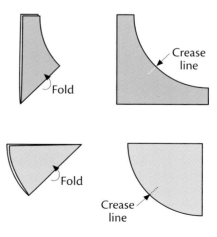

When sewing the pieces, you have the option of placing either the convex piece or the concave piece on top. I prefer placing the smallest piece on top so that I can see it, which in some situations means the convex piece is on top. This can vary according to the pattern. Feel free to experiment.

Below are some tips for successfully sewing with curves. I prefer to *not* clip the seam allowance before or after sewing, as it weakens the seam and isn't necessary. You will find that pressing the seam allowance after it's sewn will take out any distortion.

Pressing Curves

With curved piecing, there are times when it works best to press toward the curved edge and other times it's best to press away from it. In some patterns, you'll want to press the straight seams open to reduce bulk, instead of to one side. I have included specific pressing directions for each project in this book. For more pressing instructions, refer to "Quiltmaking Basics" on page 11.

Suggestions for Sewing Curves

- Set the stitch length on your machine a little longer than normal; you may find it helps when easing pieces together.

- If available, use the needle-down position on your machine. This will help keep the pieces together while you manipulate them with your hands.

- Sew slowly. Realize that you can't sew as fast when you are stitching a curved seam.

- It is essential to sew an accurate ¼" seam. Keep a seam ripper near you because you will need it more frequently when piecing curves.

- Depending on the complexity of the pattern or the number of fabrics used, I often place the pieces on a design wall and label them before sewing them together. This helps speed up the sewing process and prevents pieces of the same fabric from touching each other when I desire a scrappy look. You can make your own labels by marking small adhesive stickers. The Tag-A-Quilt printed Mylar labels available from Quilt Dance are an excellent product because they can be pinned and unpinned, allowing you to use them over and over for future projects.

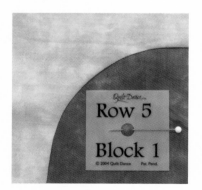

Quiltmaking Basics

In recent years, experienced quilters have become much more sophisticated in their approach to quilting. The diverse selection of fabrics, tools, and machines available to quilters today is extraordinary. Be sure to take advantage of the new techniques and tools; however, don't disregard what you already do well.

The instructions on the following pages describe the techniques that produce good results for me. Accuracy in cutting and piecing will make a big difference in curved piecing. Set a goal to enjoy the process, learn from the experience, and produce a high-quality quilt that will be treasured for years to come.

Rotary Cutting

Quilters need to understand fabric grain before they cut their fabrics. The lengthwise and crosswise grains are considered straight of grain. Bias strips are made by cutting the fabric diagonally through the straight of grain. Cutting the ends of the border and binding strips on the bias makes the seams less noticeable after the strips are sewn together. Note that rotary-cutting instructions are written for right-handers; reverse the instructions if you are left-handed.

Most of the pieces for the projects in this book can be cut using rotary-cutting techniques. I use the lines on a cutting mat and a 6" x 24" ruler to assist me in cutting accurately. Begin with fabric that has been pressed. To cut crosswise strips, fold the fabric so that the selvages meet. Lay the fabric on the cutting mat with the folded edge toward you. Fold the fabric again toward the selvage, but not all the way to the selvage. This allows you to see the selvage to make sure it remains straight, and you will not have to stretch your arms across the whole width of the fabric when cutting. Place the folded edge along any horizontal line on the mat. Place the ruler on top of the fabric along the right edge, aligning a line of the ruler with the fabric fold. The raw, uneven edges should extend beyond the ruler's edge. Place your hand firmly on the ruler and cut along the long edge of the ruler to trim off the end of the fabric, making a straight edge.

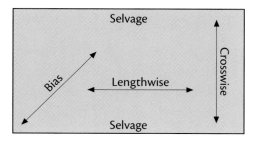

Fabric grain lines

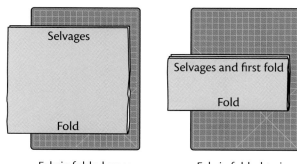

Fabric folded once   Fabric folded twice

Now, turn the fabric or mat around and place the straightened edge to your left. Cut strips the width specified in the project instructions, measuring from the straight edge. For example, if you need a 2½"-wide strip, place the 2½" line of the ruler on the straightened edge of the fabric and cut along the right edge of the ruler.

To cut squares and rectangles from a strip, unfold the cut strip once so that it is folded in half. Place the selvage edges to your right and make a cut, creating straightened edges as you did previously. Place the newly cut edges to your left. Align the proper measurement on your ruler with the straightened end of the strip and cut the fabric into squares or rectangles.

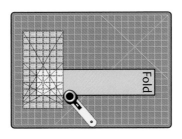

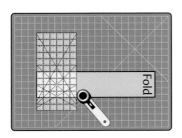

To make half-square triangles, cut the squares once diagonally.

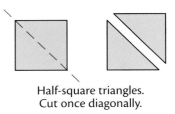

Half-square triangles.
Cut once diagonally.

Note: For instructions on rotary cutting the curved pieces using templates, refer to "Using Curved Templates" on page 8.

Making and Cutting Strip Sets

Some blocks are made by sewing strips of fabric together to make strip sets and then cutting the strip sets into segments. The segments are sewn together in a particular order to make the blocks. To make the strip sets, sew the strips together along the long edges as indicated in the project instructions. Press the seam allowances in the direction indicated. Straighten one end of the strip set, and then cut the required number of segments in the width indicated. You may need to straighten the edge periodically.

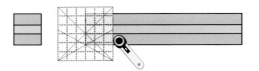

Chain Sewing

When feasible, I chain sew to decrease the time spent pulling the pieces away from the sewing machine and to reduce the amount of thread used to sew pieces together. Chain sewing involves feeding pairs of pieces under the presser foot one after another without lifting the presser foot or clipping the connecting threads. When you are finished feeding all the pieces through,

clip the threads between the units and press them as indicated in the project directions.

Pressing

Pressing is an aspect of quilting that can make a big difference in the final outcome. I recommend using a good-quality iron on a cotton setting with steam.

Before you begin pressing, consider the direction in which the seam allowances should go. Follow the directions provided for each project. Some directions suggest pressing seams open to reduce bulk, while others suggest pressing seams to one side.

When pressing seams open, you will need to turn the pieces or blocks to the wrong side and carefully open the seams with one hand while pressing with the iron in the other hand.

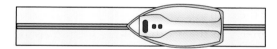

To press the seam allowance to one side, place the piece on the ironing surface with the wrong side of the fabric facing up. Press directly on the seam line of the piece while it is in the closed position. This sets the seam and helps prevent distortion.

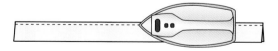

Next, open up the piece and glide the iron along the seam. This will automatically press the seam allowance toward the fabric that is on top.

Press the seam.

Finger-pressing can be a time-saver; however, I do not encourage you to take pressing shortcuts. Use the finger-pressing technique only when it's recommended in the instructions and won't interfere with the quality of the finished block.

Borders

The projects in this book provide examples of borderless quilts, quilts with simple borders, and a quilt with a pieced border, all of which are acceptable in quiltmaking. Border strips are often used to frame a quilt. When choosing a border, consider whether you want to draw attention to the quilt center or to the border. Regardless of the type of borders you apply to your quilt, your aim should be for a quilt that hangs straight and lies flat. Once the pieced center is complete, you are ready to audition fabrics for borders.

To determine the length to cut your side borders, carefully measure the length of the quilt center in three places. If the measurements are not all the same, figure the average. For example, if the three measurements are 29½", 29", and 29¼", the average would be 29¼". Cut two strips to that length.

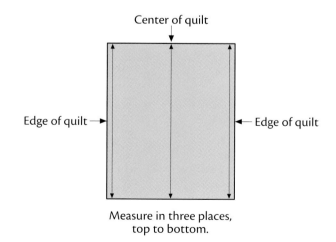

Center of quilt

Edge of quilt →   ← Edge of quilt

Measure in three places, top to bottom.

Pin-mark the center of the quilt sides. Fold each border strip in half to find the center and gently crease. Match the centers and ends of the side borders and the quilt; pin the borders to the sides, and then sew them in place. Press the seam allowances toward the borders unless otherwise instructed.

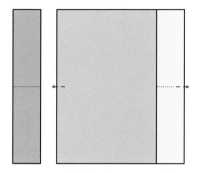

Pin the border center edge
to the quilt center edge.

Measure the width of the quilt in three places (including the just-added borders) and determine the average. Cut two border strips to this measurement. Mark the centers of the border strips and the top and bottom edges of the quilt top as before. Pin the borders to the quilt, matching the centers and the ends, and sew them in place. Press the seam allowances toward the borders unless otherwise instructed.

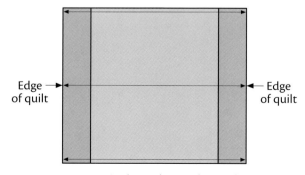

Measure in three places side to side.

Press the entire quilt. Use a square ruler to check each corner to make sure the quilt top is square. If the corners are not square, you will end up with a quilt that hangs very poorly and looks distorted. If needed, trim any slivers of fabric that are not within the squared corner.

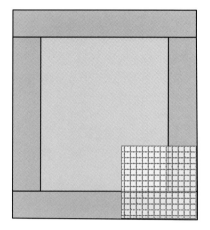

Once the quilt top is complete, take some time to clip away thread tails and fabric ears. Check for any twisted seams and make sure all the seams are pressed in the direction you intended. Re-press the entire front of the quilt. This will ensure that bulky seams or threads will not interfere with the quality of your quilting.

Backing

The backing should be 4" to 6" larger than the quilt top. In some cases you will need to piece the backing fabric to make a piece large enough. I often make pieced backings to coordinate with the front of the quilt. Avoid making a center seam, which puts undue stress down the middle of the quilt.

Batting

Many quilters enjoy selecting specific battings for their quilts depending on how the quilt will be used and the overall desired appearance. I use a medium-loft, high-quality cotton batting from Quilter's Dream for wall hangings and bed quilts. This product is exceptional for both hand and machine quilting.

Assembling the Layers

If you plan to quilt by hand or on your home sewing machine, the quilt top, batting, and backing will need to be layered and basted together. To baste, spread the backing on a large, flat surface, wrong side up. Secure the edges with masking tape. The backing should be taut but not stretched out of shape. Center the batting over the backing, smoothing out any wrinkles. Center the quilt top on the batting, right side up. Smooth out any wrinkles.

For hand quilting, baste the layers together with thread, starting at the center and working toward each corner in an X shape. Then make a grid of horizontal and vertical lines no more than 6" apart. Finish by basting around the outside edges.

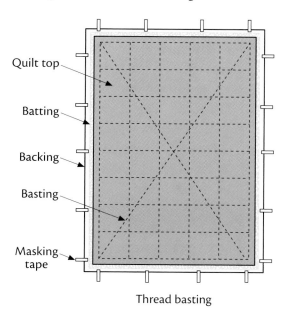

Quilt top

Batting

Backing

Basting

Masking tape

Thread basting

For machine quilting, baste the layers with No. 2 rustproof safety pins placed 3" to 4" apart.

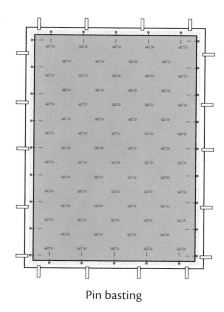

Pin basting

Quilting

Whether you plan to hand or machine quilt your project, choose high-quality thread and select a quilting design that will enhance the quilt, not detract from it. The density of quilting should be uniform throughout the entire quilt so that the quilt will not become distorted.

I enjoy free-motion designs that provide a sense of movement across the quilt. If the batik or printed fabric has a foliage or geometric design, a similar motif can be replicated in the machine quilting.

Quilts with curved piecing can end up with unavoidable bulk where the seams join. Take this into consideration when planning your quilting design.

Once the quilting is completed, take time to check the corners. If they need to be squared, use the method explained in "Borders" on page 13. Trim the backing and batting to extend ¼" beyond the quilt. This will ensure that there is batting within the binding, which helps your quilt last longer.

Binding

It is important to consider how you will finish your quilt. Adding a binding with professional techniques will yield a high-quality result. All the projects in this book have straight edges and can be bound with straight-grain, crosswise-cut, or lengthwise-cut strips.

1 Cut the specified number of 2½" strips needed for your project. Except for the beginning of the first strip and the end of the last strip, cut both ends of each strip at a 45° angle. Sew the strips together as shown to make one continuous piece, keeping the straight-cut ends at the beginning and end of the continuous strip. Press the seams to one side.

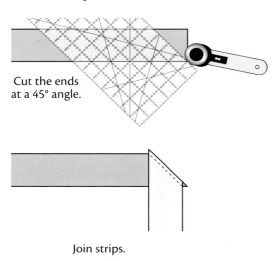

Cut the ends at a 45° angle.

Join strips.

2 Press the binding in half lengthwise, wrong sides together.

Fold

3 Place the binding on the front of the quilt several inches from a corner; align the raw edge of the binding with the raw edge of the quilt. Using a walking foot and a ¼"-wide seam, begin stitching the binding to the quilt 3" from the strip's cut end. Stop ¼" from the first corner and backstitch.

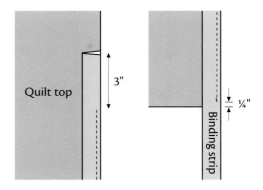

4 Remove the quilt from the sewing machine. Turn it so you are ready to sew the next edge. Fold the binding away from the quilt as shown and then fold it back down on itself to create an angled pleat at the corner. The fold should be even with the quilt top and the raw edges should be aligned. Begin with a backstitch at the fold of the binding and continue stitching until you are ¼" from the next corner. Repeat the folding and stitching process at each corner as you come to it.

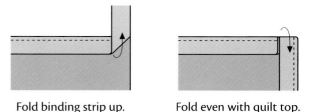

Fold binding strip up.   Fold even with quilt top.

5 Stop stitching approximately 3" from the starting end of the binding strip; backstitch. Remove the quilt from the machine. Place the quilt on a flat surface and layer the ending tail on top of the beginning tail. Trim both ends so that they are ¼" longer than needed to meet.

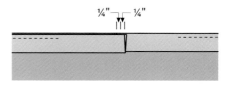

Trim ¼" longer on each end.

6 Unfold the strips and lift them away from the quilt. With right sides together, sew the ends together. Finger-press the seams to one side.

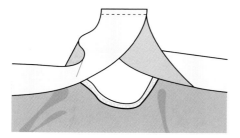

Stitch ends together.

7 Lay the binding back on the quilt, making sure it lies flat. Stitch the remaining portion of the binding to the quilt.

8 Turn the binding to the back of the quilt. Use thread that matches the binding to hand stitch the binding in place so that the folded edge covers the row of machine stitching. At each corner, fold the binding to form a miter on the back of the quilt.

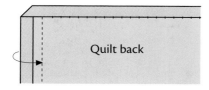

Quilt back

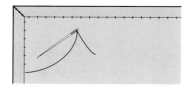

Hand stitch binding to quilt back.

Hanging Sleeves

I consider quilts to be an integral part of my home decor, so I am always looking for creative ways to display them. With a hanging sleeve attached to the back, your quilt will hang nicely from a decorative rod or flat wooden strip.

1 Cut an 8"- to 9"-wide strip of fabric long enough to span the width of your quilt. On each short end of the strip, fold over ¼" and then fold ¼" again. Press and topstitch by machine.

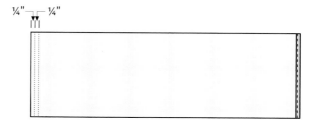

¼"   ¼"

2 Fold the strip in half lengthwise, wrong sides together. Sew a ¼" seam allowance along the long edge. Press the seam allowance to one side.

3 Press flat with the seam down the middle of the back of the tube, making a crease along the top and bottom of the tube.

4 Make an additional crease 1" from the top by folding the tube down and pressing along the length of the tube.

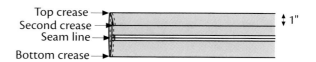

Top crease →
Second crease →   ↕ 1"
Seam line →
Bottom crease →

5 To attach the sleeve to the back of the quilt, find the center of the sleeve and lay it flat so that the top crease is just under the top binding. The second crease and the seam allowance will be facing the back of the quilt. Pin the sleeve in place, making sure it doesn't extend beyond the quilt sides. Hand stitch along the bottom crease of the sleeve to the back of the quilt. Remove the pins and fold down the top of the sleeve at the second crease. Hand stitch along the second crease. Fold the sleeve back up to the top crease, and insert the hanging rod. The rod will take up the extra space in the sleeve and allow the quilt to hang flat in the front.

Autumn Luster

Finished Quilt: 48½" x 48½" • **Finished Block: 6" x 6"**

Designed and pieced by Tammy Kelly. Machine quilted by Linda DeVries.

A combination of batiks and printed fabrics with a blending of browns, rusts, and oranges makes this large wall hanging a visual feast for fall.

Fabric-Selection Tips

In this design, I divided the quilt into quarters. After digging through my fabric stash, I decided I wanted to use similar colors to create a blended look, rather than one with high contrast. Consequently, I chose orange and rust fabrics for the four quadrants and brown for the subtle X that crisscrosses the quilt. As is typical in many of my designs, I was careful to include some each of lights, mediums, and darks to prevent a "muddy" combination of colors. I used many patterned fabrics, from geometrics to stripes, plus a few blenders to give the eye a place to rest and several metallic fabrics with a leaf motif to develop the autumn luster I was trying to achieve.

Cutting Suggestion

When cutting pieces with template B, refer to the diagram below to make best use of the fabric.

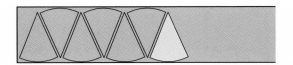

Template B cutting diagram.
Each strip yields 22 pieces.

Materials

All yardages are based on 42"-wide fabric.

¼ yard *each* of 12 assorted light to medium brown fabrics for blocks

¼ yard *each* of 15 assorted orange and rust fabrics for blocks

½ yard of orange-and-brown batik for binding

3¼ yards of fabric for backing

54" x 54" piece of batting

Cutting

All measurements include ¼"-wide seam allowances. The pattern for template B appears on page 87. For detailed instructions, refer to "Using Curved Templates" on page 8.

From *each* of 6 of the assorted light to medium brown fabrics, cut:
1 strip, 6⅞" x 42" (6 total); crosscut into 28 squares, 6⅞" x 6⅞". Cut each square once diagonally to yield 56 half-square triangles.

From *each* of the remaining 6 assorted light to medium brown fabrics, cut:
1 strip, 4" x 42" (6 total); cut 112 wedges with template B

From *each* of 8 of the assorted orange and rust fabrics, cut:
1 strip, 6⅞" x 42" (8 total); crosscut into 36 squares, 6⅞" x 6⅞". Cut each square once diagonally to yield 72 half-square triangles.

From *each* of the remaining 7 assorted orange and rust fabrics, cut:
1 strip, 4" x 42" (7 total); cut 144 wedges with template B

From the orange-and-brown batik, cut:
6 strips, 2½" x 42"

Making the Blocks

The pattern for template A appears on page 86. For detailed instructions, refer to "Using Curved Templates" on page 8.

1 Sew different brown triangles together in pairs to make 16 half-square-triangle units. Sew different orange and rust triangles together in pairs to make 24 half-square-triangle units. Then use the remaining brown triangles and orange and rust triangles to make 24 half-square-triangle units. Press the seam allowances open. Each unit should measure 6½" square.

Make 16.   Make 24.   Make 24.

2 Place template A on top of each unit from step 1 so that the line on the template is along the seam line and the straight edges of the template are even with the raw edges of the unit. Cut along the curved edges to make a total of 64 pieced A units. Discard the cutaway wedges or set them aside for a future project.

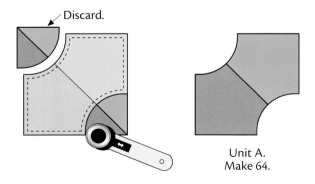

Discard.

Unit A.
Make 64.

3 Using 64 various brown B wedges, layer two different brown wedges right sides together; then sew them together to make a set. Refer to "Chain Sewing" on page 12 to make the sewing process quicker, if desired. Press the seam allowances open. Trim off the excess fabric tails. Make 32 brown wedge sets.

4 Using 96 various orange B wedges, repeat step 3 to make 48 orange wedge sets. Then, layer the 48 remaining brown wedges and 48 remaining orange wedges together in pairs. Sew 24 sets with the orange wedge on top. Sew 24 sets with the brown wedge on top. Press the seam allowances open. This will make orange-and-brown pieced wedge units that are mirror images of each other.

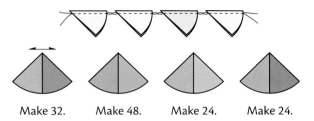

Make 32.   Make 48.   Make 24.   Make 24.

5 Use a design wall and refer to the quilt assembly diagram on page 21 to assist with your placement choices. Lay out 64 A units in eight rows of eight units each, rotating every other block 90°. Place the appropriate pieced wedge in the corner of each block. Note that the B units form a circle at the intersection of four block centers and form half circles along the outer edge of the quilt. Using the design wall before completing the blocks will allow you to make sure pieces of the same fabric are not touching each other. Once you are pleased with the arrangement, label all the blocks so that you'll know where to place them after sewing and pressing.

6 Place a pieced B wedge on top of an A unit as shown, right sides together, and match the center seams. Place a pin through the center of each piece and at each end as shown. With the B wedge on top, sew the pieces together along the curved edge, easing to fit. Press the seam allowances

toward the pieced corner wedge. Repeat to sew a pieced wedge on the opposite corner. The block should measure 6½" square. Make a total of 64 blocks.

Make 64.

Assembling the Quilt Top

1 Return the completed blocks to your design wall and carefully examine the layout to make sure that each block is placed correctly.

2 Sew the blocks in each row together, matching seams carefully. Press the seam allowances open.

3 Join the rows to complete the quilt top. Press the seam allowances open. Press the entire quilt top.

Finishing the Quilt

Refer to "Quiltmaking Basics" on page 11 as needed to complete the following steps.

1 Layer the quilt top with the batting and backing. Baste the layers together.

2 Hand or machine quilt as desired.

3 Square up the quilt sandwich if needed.

4 Prepare the orange-and-brown batik binding and sew it to the quilt. Add a hanging sleeve, if desired.

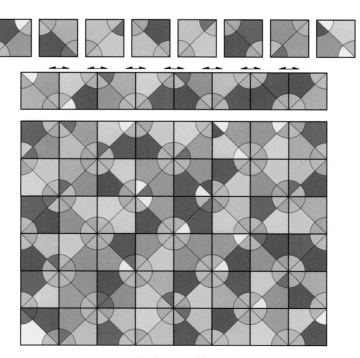

Quilt assembly

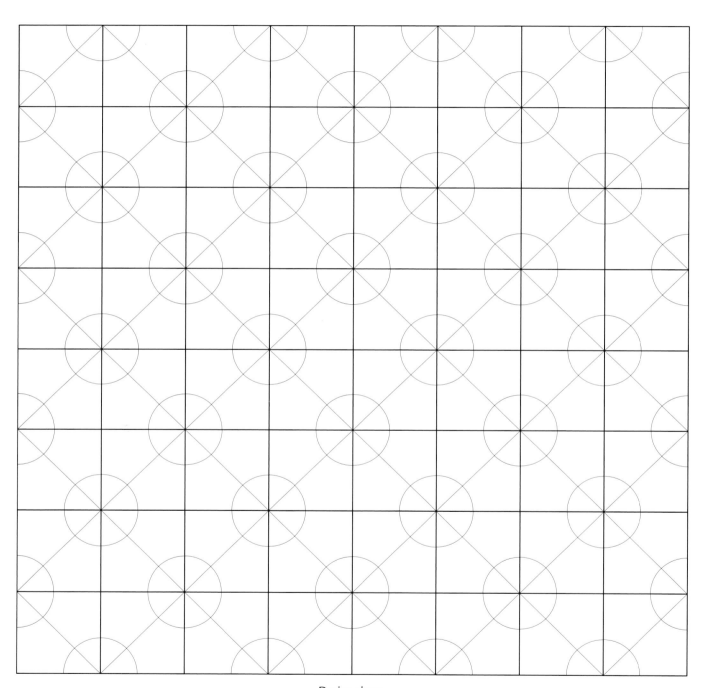

Design sheet

Sea Dreams

Finished Quilt: 48½" x 48½" • **Finished Block:** 6" x 6"

Designed and pieced by Tammy Kelly. Machine quilted by Linda DeVries.

The aquamarine and violet batiks of this large wall hanging remind me of an underwater adventure, and a flowing machine-quilted seaweed motif completes the effect.

Fabric-Selection Tips

I chose to develop an analogous color plan for this quilt design, drawing on hues ranging from violet to green. One light and one medium violet fabric along with one light and one medium green fabric were selected to make the triangle wedges consistent and come full circle. Many varied aqua and violet fabrics were chosen for the large pieces and placed together to look like a solid shape. The variety of prints in the batiks, including dots, foliage prints, florals, and swirls, adds movement and depth.

Cutting Suggestion

When cutting the pieces with template B, refer to the diagram on page 19 to make the best use of the fabric.

Materials

All yardages are based on 42"-wide fabric.

½ yard *each* of 7 assorted aqua and violet batiks for blocks

½ yard of light purple batik for blocks

½ yard of medium purple batik for blocks

½ yard of light green batik for blocks

½ yard of medium green batik for blocks

½ yard of aqua batik for binding

3¼ yards of fabric for backing

54" x 54" piece of batting

Cutting

All measurements include ¼"-wide seam allowances. The pattern for template B appears on page 87. For detailed instructions, refer to "Using Curved Templates" on page 8.

From *each* of the 7 assorted aqua and violet batiks, cut:

2 strips, 6⅞" x 42" (14 total); crosscut into 64 squares, 6⅞" x 6⅞". Cut each square once diagonally to yield 128 half-square triangles.

From the light purple batik, cut:

3 strips, 4" x 42"; cut 64 wedges with template B

From the medium purple batik, cut:

3 strips, 4" x 42"; cut 64 wedges with template B

From the light green batik, cut:

3 strips, 4" x 42"; cut 64 wedges with template B

From the medium green batik, cut:

3 strips, 4" x 42"; cut 64 wedges with template B

From the aqua batik for binding, cut:

6 strips, 2½" x 42"

Making the Blocks

The pattern for template A appears on page 86. For detailed instructions, refer to "Using Curved Templates" on page 8.

1 Select four matching aqua or violet triangles and sew them to a different aqua or violet triangle to make four half-square-triangle units. Press the seam allowances open. Each unit should measure 6½" square. Repeat to make a total of 64 half-square-triangle units.

Make 64.

2 Place template A on top of each unit from step 1 so that the line on the template is along the seam line and the straight edges of the template are even with the raw edges of the unit. Cut along the curved edges to mak e a total of 64 pieced A units. Discard the cutaway wedges or set them aside for a future project.

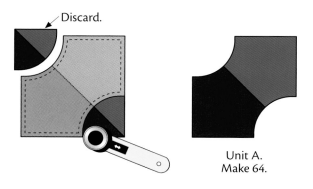

Discard.

Unit A.
Make 64.

3 Using the 64 light purple and 64 medium purple B wedges, with right sides together, sew a light purple B wedge to a medium purple B wedge to form a set, making sure the same fabric is always on top. Refer to "Chain Sewing" on page 12 to make the sewing process quicker, if desired. Press the seam allowances open. Trim off the excess fabric tails. Make 64 purple wedge sets. Using the 64 light green and 64 medium green wedges, repeat to make 64 green wedge sets.

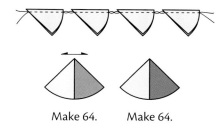

Make 64.   Make 64.

4 Use a design wall and refer to the quilt assembly diagram on page 26 to assist with your placement choices. Lay out the 64 A units in eight rows of eight units each, rotating every other block 90°. Place the appropriate pieced wedge in the corner of each block. Note that the B units form a circle at the intersection of four block centers and form half circles along the outer edge of the quilt. Once you are pleased with the arrangement, label all the blocks so that you'll know where to place them after sewing and pressing.

5 Place a pieced B wedge on top of an A unit as shown, right sides together, and match the center seams. Place a pin through the center of each piece and at each end as shown. With the B wedge on top, sew the pieces together along the curved edge, easing to fit. Press the seam allowances toward the pieced corner wedge. Repeat to sew a pieced wedge on the opposite corner. The block should measure 6½" square. Repeat to make a total of 64 blocks.

Make 64.

Assembling the Quilt Top

1 Return the completed blocks to your design wall and carefully examine the layout to make sure that each block is placed correctly.

2 Sew the blocks in each row together, matching seams carefully. Press the seam allowances open.

3 Join the rows to complete the quilt top. Press the seam allowances open. Press the entire quilt top.

Finishing the Quilt

Refer to "Quiltmaking Basics" on page 11 as needed to complete the following steps.

1 Layer the quilt top with the batting and backing. Baste the layers together.

2 Hand or machine quilt as desired.

3 Square up the quilt sandwich if needed.

4 Prepare the aqua batik binding and sew it to the quilt. Add a hanging sleeve, if desired.

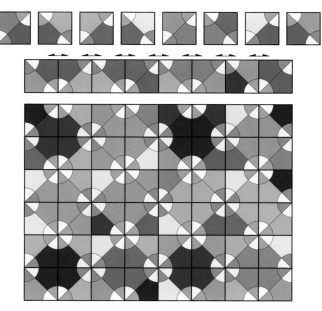

Quilt assembly

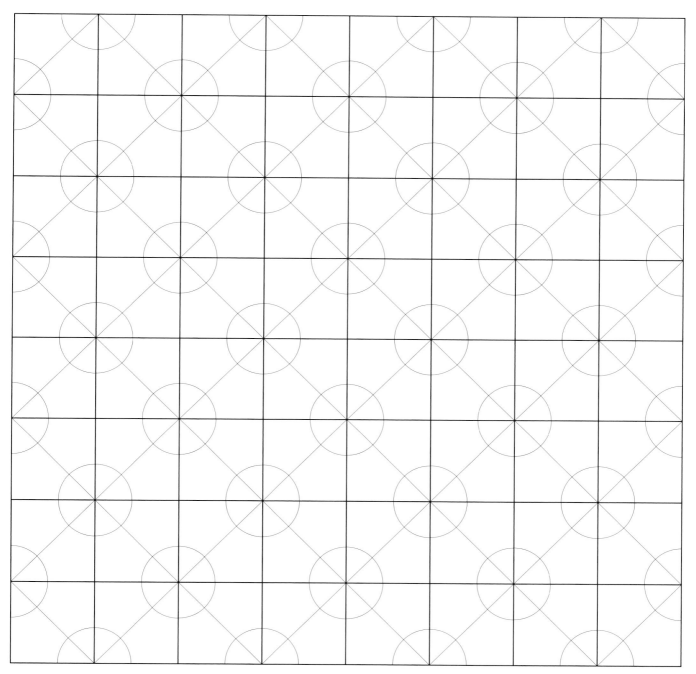

Design sheet

Mesmerize

Finished Quilt: 60½" x 60½" • Finished Block: 6" x 6"

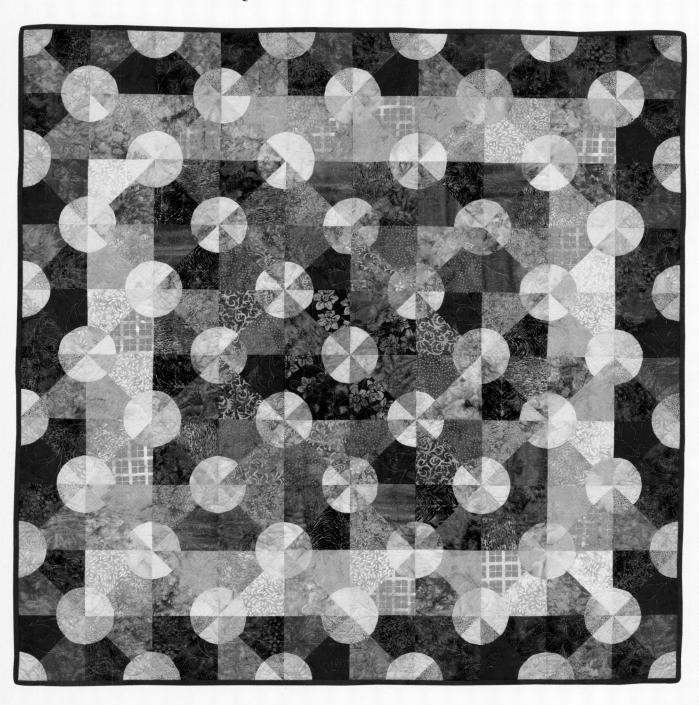

Designed and pieced by Tammy Kelly. Machine quilted by Linda DeVries.

A masterpiece of color! This is my interpretation of a color wheel in fabric. This large wall hanging uses 48 varied batik fabrics encompassing a full spectrum, including magenta, yellow, orange, green, blue, and reddish violet.

Fabric-Selection Tips

I chose medium to very dark batik fabrics for the large pieces in this project. They contrast well with the very light batiks used for the wedges. The light wedges also create a bridge from one row of color to the next. Notice how the dark magenta frames the quilt, yet your eye is also drawn through the gradation of colors to the quilt center. To develop high interest, the batiks vary from florals, foliage, and plaids to almost solids.

Cutting Suggestion

When cutting the pieces with template B, refer to the diagram on page 19 to make the best use of the fabric.

Materials

All yardages are based on 42"-wide fabric.

¼ yard *each* of 8 assorted medium to dark pink batiks for blocks

¼ yard *each* of 7 assorted light pink batiks for blocks

¼ yard *each* of 6 assorted medium to dark yellow or orange batiks for blocks

¼ yard *each* of 6 assorted light yellow batiks for blocks

¼ yard *each* of 4 assorted medium to dark green batiks for blocks

¼ yard *each* of 4 assorted light green batiks for blocks

¼ yard *each* of 3 assorted medium to dark blue batiks for blocks

¼ yard *each* of 3 assorted light blue batiks for blocks

¼ yard *each* of 3 assorted medium to dark reddish violet batiks for blocks

¼ yard *each* of 3 assorted light reddish violet batiks for blocks

⅝ yard of dark magenta batik for binding

4¼ yards of fabric for backing

66" x 66" piece of batting

Cutting

All measurements include ¼"-wide seam allowances. The pattern for template B appears on page 87. For detailed instructions, refer to "Using Curved Templates" on page 8.

From *each* of the 8 assorted medium to dark pink batiks, cut:

1 strip, 6⅞" x 42" (8 total); crosscut into 36 squares, 6⅞" x 6⅞". Cut each square once diagonally to yield 72 half-square triangles.

From *each* of the 6 assorted medium to dark yellow or orange batiks, cut:

1 strip, 6⅞" x 42" (6 total); crosscut into 28 squares, 6⅞" x 6⅞". Cut each square once diagonally to yield 56 half-square triangles.

From *each* of the 4 assorted medium to dark green batiks, cut:

1 strip, 6⅞" x 42" (4 total); crosscut into 20 squares, 6⅞" x 6⅞". Cut each square once diagonally to yield 40 half-square triangles.

From the 3 assorted medium to dark blue batiks, cut a *total* of:

12 assorted squares, 6⅞" x 6⅞"; cut each square once diagonally to yield 24 half-square triangles

From the 3 assorted medium to dark reddish violet batiks, cut a *total* of:

4 squares, 6⅞" x 6⅞"; cut each square once diagonally to yield 8 half-square triangles

From *each* of the 7 assorted light pink batiks, cut:

1 strip, 4" x 42" (7 total); cut a total of 144 wedges with template B

From *each* of the 6 assorted light yellow batiks, cut:

1 strip, 4" x 42" (6 total); cut a total of 112 wedges with template B

From *each* of the 4 assorted light green batiks, cut:

1 strip, 4" x 42" (4 total); cut a total of 80 wedges with template B

From *each* of the 3 assorted light blue batiks, cut:

1 strip, 4" x 42" (3 total); cut a total of 48 wedges with template B

From *each* of the 3 assorted light reddish violet batiks, cut:

1 strip, 4" x 42" (3 total); cut a total of 16 wedges with template B

From the dark magenta batik, cut:

7 strips, 2½" x 42"

Making the Blocks

The pattern for template A appears on page 86. For detailed instructions, refer to "Using Curved Templates" on page 8.

1   Sew two different triangles from the same color family together to make a half-square-triangle unit. Press the seam allowances open. Each unit should measure 6½" square. Make the number indicated for each color family.

Make 36.

Make 28.

Make 20.

Make 12.

Make 4.

2 Place template A on top of each unit from step 1 so that the line on the template is along the seam line and the straight edges of the template are even with the raw edges of the unit. Cut along the curved edges to make a total of 100 A units. Discard the cutaway wedges or set them aside for a future project.

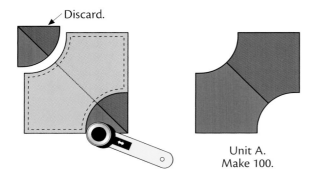

Unit A.
Make 100.

3 Using the B wedges, layer two different wedges from the same color family right sides together; then sew the wedges in pairs to make a set. Refer to "Chain Sewing" on page 12 to make the sewing process quicker, if desired. Press the seam allowances open. Trim off the excess fabric tails. Make the number indicated for each color family.

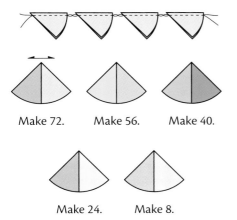

Make 72.   Make 56.   Make 40.

Make 24.   Make 8.

4 Use a design wall and refer to the quilt assembly diagram on page 32 to assist with your placement choices. Lay out the 100 A units in 10 rows of 10 units each, rotating every other block 90°. Place the appropriate pieced wedge in the corner of each block. Note that the B units form a circle at the intersection of four block centers and form half circles along the outer edge of the quilt. Using the design wall before completing the blocks will allow you to make sure pieces of the same fabric are not touching each other. Once you are pleased with the arrangement, label all the blocks so that you'll know where to place them after sewing and pressing.

5 Place a pieced B wedge on top of an A unit as shown, right sides together, and match the center seams. Place a pin through the center of each piece and at each end as shown. With the B wedge on top, sew the pieces together along the curved edge, easing to fit. Press the seam allowances toward the wedge set. Repeat to sew a pieced wedge on the opposite corner. The blocks should measure 6½" square. Make a total of 100 blocks.

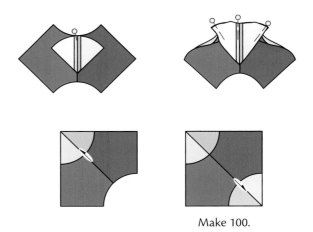

Make 100.

Assembling the Quilt Top

1 Return the completed blocks to your design wall and carefully examine the layout to make sure that each block is placed correctly.

2 Sew the blocks in each row together, matching seams carefully. Press the seam allowances open.

3 Join the rows to complete the quilt top. Press the seam allowances open. Press the entire quilt top.

Finishing the Quilt

Refer to "Quiltmaking Basics" on page 11 as needed to complete the following steps.

1 Layer the quilt top with the batting and backing. Baste the layers together.

2 Hand or machine quilt as desired.

3 Square up the quilt sandwich if needed.

4 Prepare the dark magenta binding and sew it to the quilt. Add a hanging sleeve, if desired.

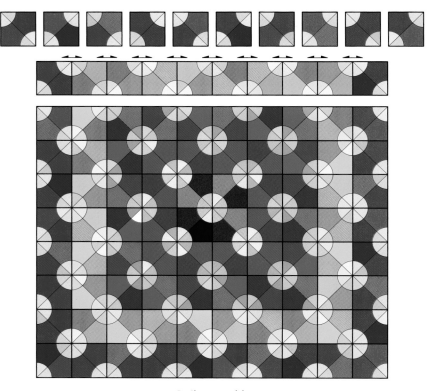

Quilt assembly

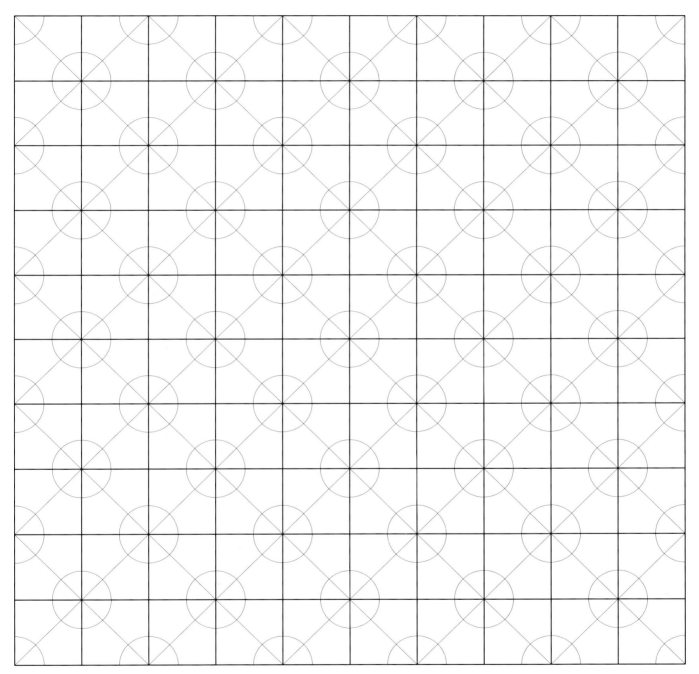

Design sheet

Stars 'n' Curves

Finished Quilt: 51" x 51"

Designed and pieced by Tammy Kelly. Machine quilted by Linda DeVries.

An interesting geometric print fabric in terra-cotta red, purple, gold, and green is the focal point in this eye-catching wall hanging. I've combined variations of the traditional Sawtooth Star and Drunkard's Path designs to create this charming quilt.

Fabric-Selection Tips

The multicolored large-scale print of the geometric fabric is bold, yet it poses as a medium value. I chose a mottled beige for the background of the large blocks to create the contrast and soften the curved edges. A medium gold contrasts well with the dark purple, green, and red Sawtooth Stars. I still wanted the geometric print to take center stage, so I separated the stars with four large rectangles of the focus fabric. A pieced inner border adds charm and brightness to the piece. The outer border is purposely subtle to draw the eye to the quilt center.

Cutting Suggestions

When cutting the pieces with templates C and D, refer to the diagrams below to make the best use of the fabric.

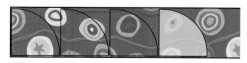

Template C cutting diagram.
Each strip yields 10 pieces.

Template D cutting diagram.
Each strip yields 12 pieces.

Materials

All yardages are based on 42"-wide fabric.

1⅜ yards of multicolored geometric print for blocks and binding

1¼ yards *total* of 3 similar medium gold fabrics for blocks and borders

⅞ yard of light gold fabric for blocks

⅜ yard *each* of medium green, dark green, medium purple, and dark purple fabrics for blocks and inner border

¼ yard of dark red fabric for center block and inner border

5" square of medium red fabric for center block

3½ yards of fabric for backing

57" x 57" piece of batting

Cutting

All measurements include ¼"-wide seam allowances. The patterns for templates C and D appear on page 87. For detailed instructions, refer to "Using Curved Templates" on page 8.

From the multicolored geometric print, cut:

1 strip, 12½" x 42"; crosscut into four rectangles, 8½" x 12½"

4 strips, 4" x 42"; cut 40 pieces with template C

6 strips, 2½" x 42"

From *each* of the medium green, dark green, medium purple, and dark purple fabrics, cut:

1 square, 4½" x 4½" (4 total)

1 strip, 2⅞" x 14"; crosscut into 4 squares, 2⅞" x 2⅞" (16 total). Cut each square once diagonally to yield 32 half-square triangles.

1 strip (4 total) in varied widths from 1" to 3" x 42"; crosscut each strip into 4 equal lengths

From the dark red fabric, cut:

1 strip, 2⅞" x 14"; crosscut into 4 squares, 2⅞" x 2⅞". Cut each square once diagonally to yield 8 half-square triangles.

1 strip, 2" x 42"; crosscut into 4 equal lengths

From the medium red fabric, cut:

1 square, 4½" x 4½"

From the 3 similar medium gold fabrics, cut a *total* of:

5 strips, 4½" x 42"

2 strips, 2⅞" x 42"; crosscut into 20 squares, 2⅞" x 2⅞". Cut each square once diagonally to yield 40 half-square triangles.

2 strips, 2½" x 42"; crosscut into 20 squares, 2½" x 2½"

2 strips in different widths from 1½" to 2½" x 42"; crosscut each strip into 4 equal lengths

From the light gold fabric, cut:

2 strips, 4½" x 42"; crosscut into 16 squares, 4½" x 4½"

4 strips, 4½" x 42"; cut 40 pieces with template D

Making the Blocks

1 To make the Sawtooth Star blocks, sew a green, purple, or red triangle to each medium gold triangle to make a half-square-triangle unit. Refer to "Chain Sewing" on page 12 to make the sewing process quicker, if desired. Press the seam allowances toward the darker fabric. Make the number indicated for each color combination.

Make 8.   Make 8.   Make 8.   Make 8.   Make 8.

2 Arrange four 2½" medium gold squares, eight matching half-square-triangle units from step 1, and one 4½" square in rows as shown. Sew the units in each row together. Press the seam allowances as shown. Sew the rows together. Press the seam allowances toward the center square. The Sawtooth Star block should measure 8½" square. Repeat to make a total of two green blocks, two purple blocks, and one red block.

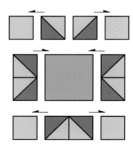 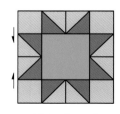

Make 5 total.

3 To make the pieced curved units, place a light gold D piece on top of each geometric print C piece, right sides together, and match the center marks. Place a pin through the center of each piece and at each end, matching the end marks. With the D piece on top, sew the pieces together along the curved edge, easing to fit as needed. Press the seam allowances toward the D piece. Make a total of 40 curved units.

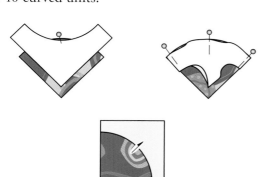

Make 40.

4 Arrange a green or purple Sawtooth Star block, eight curved units, and four 4½" light gold squares in rows. Sew the units in each row together as shown. Press the seam allowances as shown. Sew the rows together. Press the seam allowances as shown. The block should measure 16½" square. Make two green blocks and two purple blocks.

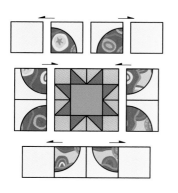

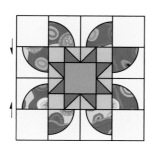

Make 2 green and
2 purple (4 total).

5 Sew two curved units together as shown and press seam allowances in one direction. Then sew them to the short end of an 8½" x 12½" geometric print rectangle; press. Repeat to make a total of four rectangle units.

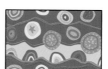 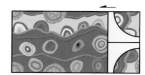

Make 4.

Assembling the Quilt Top

1 Arrange the green blocks, purple blocks, four rectangle units, and the red Sawtooth Star block in three horizontal rows as shown below.

2 Sew the pieces in each row together. Press the seam allowances toward the rectangles.

3 Sew the rows together. Press the seam allowances in one direction. Press the entire quilt center. The quilt center should measure 40½" square.

Adding the Borders

1. To make the pieced inner border, randomly sew the 2"-wide red strips and the various widths of medium gold, dark green, dark purple, medium green, and medium purple strips together until you have a strip set that measures 10" x 45". Press all seam allowances in one direction. Cut the strip set into four segments, 1¾" wide.

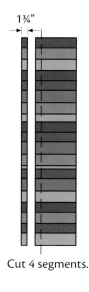

1¾"

Cut 4 segments.

2. Referring to "Borders" on page 13, measure the sides of your quilt and trim two segments from step 1 to that measurement. Sew the trimmed segments to the top and bottom of the quilt center. Press the seam allowances toward the borders. Measure the width of your quilt, including the just-added borders, and trim two segments from step 1 to that measurement. Sew the trimmed segments to the sides of the quilt center and press.

3. Sew the 4½" medium gold strips together end to end to make one long strip. Refer to "Borders" to measure, cut, and sew the medium gold strips to the quilt top. Press the seam allowances toward the outer-border strips. Press the entire quilt top.

Quilt assembly

Finishing the Quilt

Refer to "Quiltmaking Basics" on page 11 as needed to complete the following steps.

1 Layer the quilt top with the batting and backing. Baste the layers together.

2 Hand or machine quilt as desired.

3 Square up the quilt sandwich if needed.

4 Prepare the geometric print binding and sew it to the quilt. Add a hanging sleeve, if desired.

Design sheet

Splish Splash!

Finished Quilt: 45" x 45"

Designed and pieced by Tammy Kelly. Machine quilted by Linda DeVries.

The combination of Four Patch blocks and curved piecing replicates the traditional Pictures in the Stairwell block. A unique selection of contemporary fabrics will make this midsize wall hanging a central attraction in any room.

Fabric-Selection Tips

The fabric selections incorporate an analogous color plan ranging from lime green to aqua to purple. Several of the blue hand-dyed fabrics resemble water. The purple squares are from four blender fabrics. The lightest green fabric has a hint of yellow, which provides contrast and coordinates nicely with the spectacular large-scale batik border. The Four Patch corner blocks are a simple duplication from the quilt center, yet they give the quilt a look of completion.

Cutting Suggestion

When cutting the pieces with templates C and D, refer to the diagram on page 35 to make the best use of the fabric.

Materials

All yardages are based on 42"-wide fabric.

⅞ yard of blue-and-green large-scale batik for outer border

⅝ yard of dark purple batik for inner border and binding

½ yard of green batik for blocks

¼ yard *each* of 4 assorted purple fabrics for blocks and border corner squares

¼ yard *each* of 4 assorted medium to dark blue fabrics for blocks

⅛ yard *each* of 4 assorted green fabrics for blocks

3⅛ yards of fabric for backing

51" x 51" piece of batting

Cutting

All measurements include ¼" wide seam allowances. The patterns for templates C and D appear on page 87. For detailed instructions, refer to "Using Curved Templates" on page 8.

From *each* of the 4 assorted green fabrics, cut:
1 strip, 2½" x 42" (4 total)

From *each* of the 4 assorted purple fabrics, cut:
1 strip, 2½" x 42" (4 total)
1 strip, 3¼" x 14" (4 total)

From the green batik, cut:
3 strips, 4½" x 42"; cut 32 pieces with template D

From *each* of the 4 assorted medium to dark blue fabrics, cut:
1 strip, 4" x 42" (4 total); cut a total of 32 pieces with template C

From the dark purple batik, cut:

4 strips, 1¼" x 42"

5 strips, 2½" x 42"

From the blue-and-green large-scale batik, cut:

4 strips, 6" x 42"

Making the Blocks

1. To make the four-patch units, sew a 2½" x 42" purple strip to one long edge of a 2½" x 42" green strip to make a strip set. Press the seam allowances toward the purple fabric. Repeat to make four strip sets. Crosscut each strip set into 16 segments (64 total), 2½" wide.

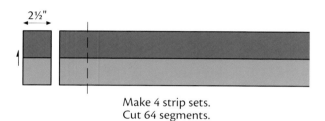

Make 4 strip sets.
Cut 64 segments.

2. Randomly sew two segments from step 1 together; be sure the segments are not matching. Press the seam allowances to one side to complete a four-patch unit. The unit should measure 4½" square. Make 32 units.

Make 32.

3. To make the pieced curved units, place a green D piece on top of each blue C piece, right sides together, and match the center marks. Place a pin through the center of each piece and at each end, matching the end marks. With the D piece

on top, sew the pieces together along the curved edge, easing to fit as needed. Press the seam allowances toward the D piece. Make 32 curved units.

Make 32 .

Assembling the Quilt Top

1. Arrange the four-patch units and the curved units in eight horizontal rows of eight units each, alternating the units in each row and from row to row as shown in the diagram following step 3.

2. Sew the units in each row together. Press the seam allowances in alternate directions from row to row.

3. Sew the rows together. Press the seam allowances in one direction. Press the entire quilt center. The quilt center should measure 32½" square.

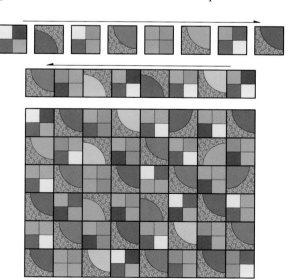

Adding the Borders

1 Referring to "Borders" on page 13, measure, cut, and sew the 1¼"-wide dark purple strips to the quilt center. Press the seam allowances toward the border strips.

2 To make the border corner blocks, sew two 3¼" x 14" purple strips together along one long edge to make a strip set. Press the seam allowances toward one strip. Make two strip sets. Crosscut each strip set into four segments (eight total), 3¼" wide.

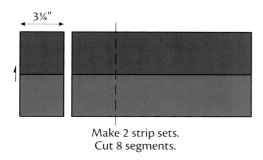

Make 2 strip sets.
Cut 8 segments.

3 Sew two different segments from step 2 together to make a Four Patch block. Press the seam allowances to one side. The block should measure 6" square. Make four blocks.

Make 4.

4 Refer to "Borders" to measure the sides of your quilt. Trim the four 6"-wide blue-and-green batik strips to that measurement. Sew two of the strips to the sides of the quilt center. Press the seam

allowances toward the outer-border strips. Sew a purple Four Patch block from step 3 to each end of the two remaining border strips and sew them to the top and bottom of the quilt center. Press the entire quilt top.

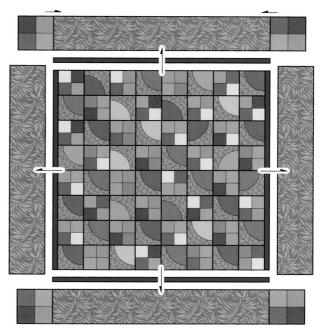

Quilt assembly

Finishing the Quilt

Refer to "Quiltmaking Basics" on page 11 as needed to complete the following steps.

1 Layer the quilt top with the batting and backing. Baste the layers together.

2 Hand or machine quilt as desired.

3 Square up the quilt sandwich if needed.

4 Prepare the dark purple binding and sew it to the quilt. Add a hanging sleeve, if desired.

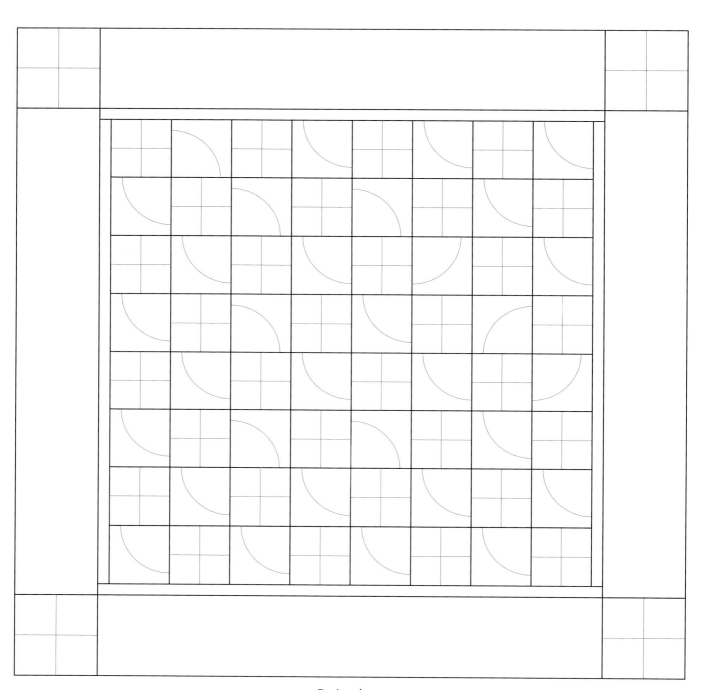

Design sheet

Bits of Shimmer

Finished Quilt: 65½" x 97½" • **Finished Block: 16" x 16"**

Designed and pieced by Tammy Kelly. Machine quilted by Linda DeVries.

Inspired by a vintage 1930s quilt design called Mohawk Trail, this twin-size quilt can easily be adapted to any bed size. The quarter circle is split in half in this scrappy version of the classic Drunkard's Path design.

Fabric-Selection Tips

As is customary with many of my quilts, I wanted to have a representation of light, medium, and dark fabrics in "Bits of Shimmer." To establish the contrast, the shimmering frosted lavender fabric chosen for the light background is combined with various purples and greens in medium to dark values. Splitting the quarter circles creates an opportunity to include a scrappy variety of purples and greens in prints, batiks, and blender fabrics. A polka-dot inner border, batik middle border, and frosted outer border complete this predominantly purple project.

Cutting Suggestion

When cutting the pieces with template D, refer to the diagram on page 35 to make the best use of the fabric.

Materials

All yardages are based on 42"-wide fabric.

2⅞ yards of frosted light purple fabric for blocks

2⅝ yards of frosted medium purple fabric for outer border

1 yard of purple batik for middle border and binding

½ yard of purple polka-dot fabric for inner border

¼ yard *each* of 14 assorted purple fabrics for blocks

¼ yard *each* of 13 assorted green fabrics for blocks

6⅜ yards of fabric for backing

72" x 104" piece of batting

Cutting

All measurements include ¼"-wide seam allowances. The pattern for template D appears on page 87. For detailed instructions, refer to "Using Curved Templates" on page 8.

From *each* of the 14 assorted purple fabrics, cut:
1 strip, 4⅜" x 42"; crosscut into 9 squares (126 total), 4⅜" x 4⅜". Cut each square once diagonally to yield 252 half-square triangles.

From *each* of the 13 assorted green fabrics, cut:
1 strip, 4⅜" x 42"; crosscut into 9 squares (117 total), 4⅜" x 4⅜". Cut each square once diagonally to yield 234 half-square triangles.

From the frosted light purple fabric, cut:
20 strips, 4½" x 42"; cut 240 pieces with template D

From the purple polka-dot fabric, cut:
7 strips, 2" x 42"

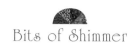

From the purple batik, cut:
7 strips, 1¼" x 42"

9 strips, 2½" x 42"

From the frosted medium purple fabric, cut on the *lengthwise* grain:
4 strips, 6¾" x 88"

Making the Blocks

The pattern for template C appears on page 87. For detailed instructions, refer to "Using Curved Templates" on page 8.

1 To make the pieced quarter circles, start by sewing two triangles together to make a half-square-triangle unit. Note that some units will have two purple triangles and others will have a purple and a green triangle. Refer to "Chain Sewing" on page 12 to make the sewing process quicker, if desired. Press the seam allowances open. Make 240 units. You'll have six extra triangles. Discard or set them aside for a future project.

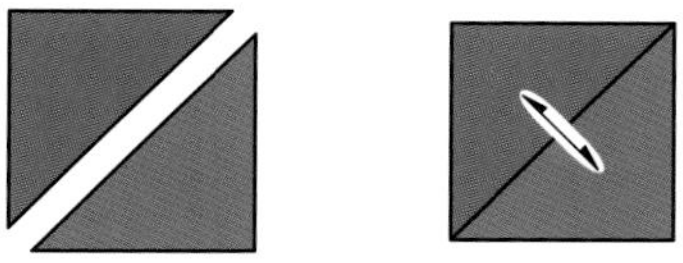

Make 240.

2 Place template C on top of each unit from step 1, making sure the seam is aligned with the line on the template and the straight edges of the template are even with the raw edges of the unit. Cut along the curved edge to make a total of 240 pieced C units. Discard the remaining fabric.

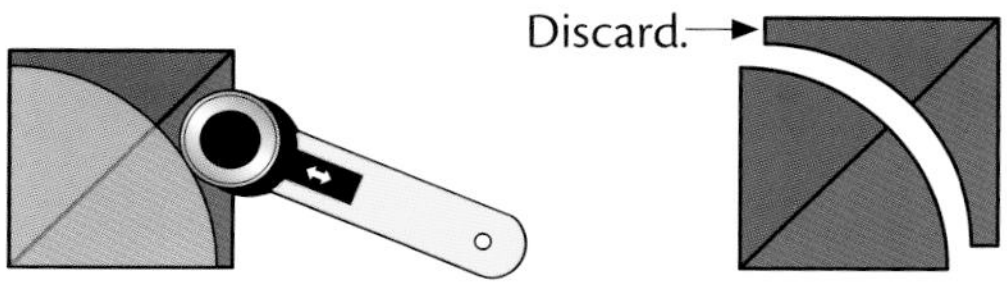

Make 240.

3 To make the curved units, place a light purple D piece on top of each pieced C unit from step 2, right sides together, and match the center marks. Place a pin through the center of each piece and at each end, matching the end marks. With the D piece on top, sew the pieces together along the curved edges, easing to fit as needed. Press the seam allowances toward the D piece. Make a total of 240 curved units.

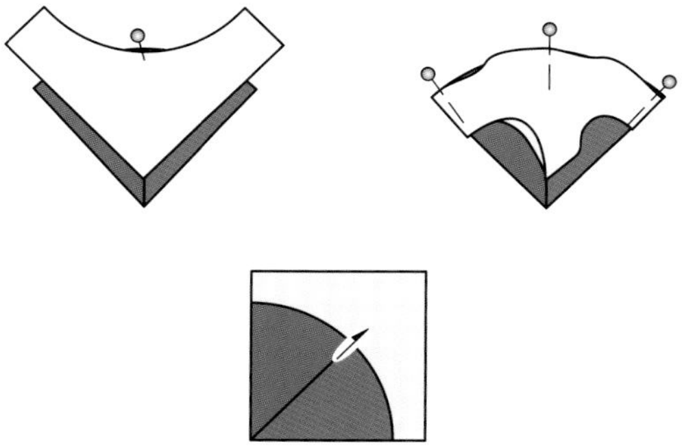

Make 240.

4 Arrange 16 curved units in four rows as shown. Sew the units in each row together. Press the seam allowances in alternating directions from row to row. Sew the rows together; press. The block should measure 16½" square. Make 15 blocks.

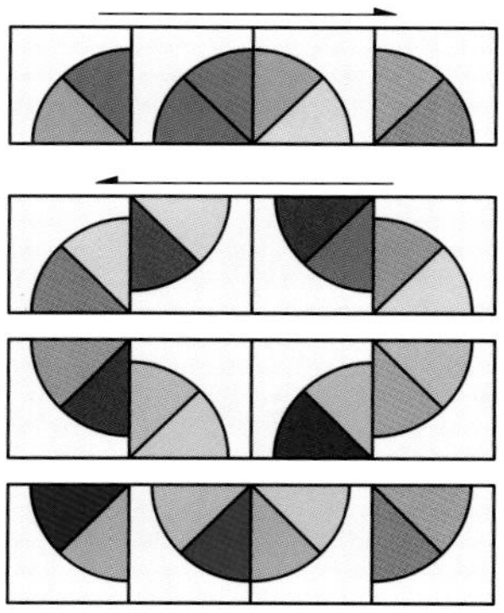

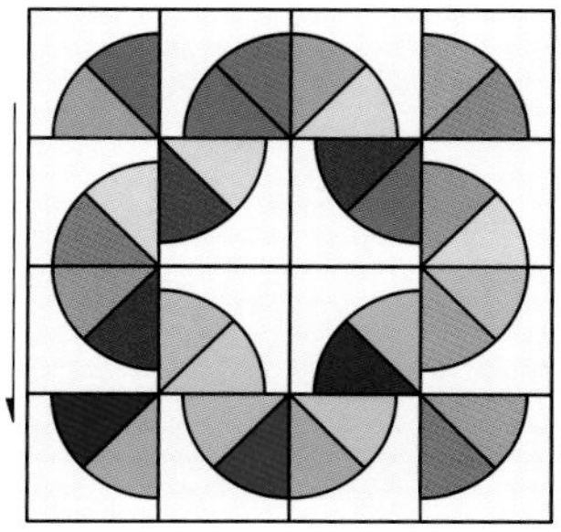

Make 15.

Assembling the Quilt Top

1. Arrange the blocks in five horizontal rows of three blocks each.

2. Sew the blocks in each row together. Press the seam allowances in alternate directions from row to row.

3. Sew the rows together. Press the seam allowances in one direction. Press the entire quilt center. The quilt center should measure 48½" x 80½".

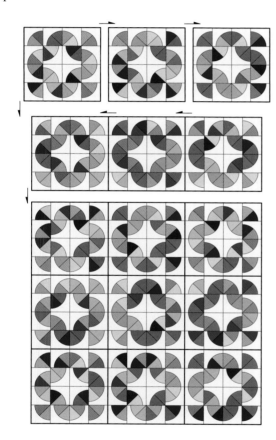

Adding the Borders

1. Sew the 2"-wide purple polka-dot strips together end to end to make one long strip. Sew the 1¼"-wide purple batik strips together end to end to make one long strip.

2. Referring to "Borders" on page 13, measure, cut, and sew the polka-dot inner-border strips, then the purple batik middle-border strips, and lastly the 6¾"-wide frosted medium purple strips to the quilt top. Press all seam allowances away from the center. Press the entire quilt top.

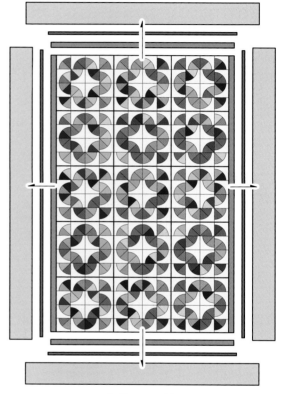

Quilt assembly

Finishing the Quilt

Refer to "Quiltmaking Basics" on page 11 as needed to complete the following steps.

1. Layer the quilt top with the batting and backing. Baste the layers together.

2. Hand or machine quilt as desired.

3. Square up the quilt sandwich if needed.

4. Prepare the purple batik binding and sew it to the quilt. Add a hanging sleeve, if desired.

Design sheet

Melon Patch

Finished Quilt: 35" x 35" ● **Block Size: 4" x 4"**

Designed and pieced by Tammy Kelly. Machine quilted by Linda DeVries.

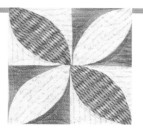

Metallic gold and green add a touch of elegance to this small wall hanging or table centerpiece. It's a simple two-color quilt design that is sometimes known by the name Orange Peel.

Fabric-Selection Tips

The cream background fabric, featuring an elegant print of antique script, contrasts well with the mossy green selections. Using two different green fabrics adds interest, especially because the basket-weave print creates a diagonal stripe. A narrow border in a slightly darker shade of green was chosen to frame the quilt center. The metallic gold-and-green fabric is repeated in the outer border and binding, which allows the eye to be drawn to the curved piecing.

Cutting Suggestions

When cutting the pieces with templates E and F, refer to the diagram below to make the best use of the fabric.

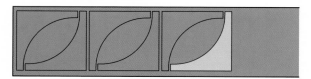

Template E cutting diagram.
1 strip yields 14 pieces.

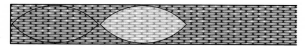

Template F cutting diagram.
1 strip yields 6 pieces.

Materials

All yardages are based on 42"-wide fabric.

1½ yards of metallic gold-and-green fabric for blocks, outer border, and binding

⅞ yard of cream print for blocks

⅓ yard of medium green print for blocks

⅛ yard medium green solid for inner border

1⅓ yards of fabric for backing

41" x 41" piece of batting

Cutting

All measurements include ¼"-wide seam allowances. The patterns for templates E and F appear on page 88. For detailed instructions, refer to "Using Curved Templates" on page 8.

From the cream print, cut:

3 strips, 5¼" x 42"; cut 36 pieces with template E

3 strips, 3" x 42"; cut 18 pieces with template F

From the metallic gold-and-green fabric, cut:

7 strips, 5¼" x 42"; from *3 of the strips,* cut 36 pieces with template E

4 strips, 2½" x 42"

From the medium green print, cut:

3 strips, 3" x 42"; cut 18 pieces with template F

From the medium green solid, cut:

3 strips, 1" x 42"

Making the Blocks

1 To make the pieced curved units, place a metallic gold-and-green E piece on top of a cream F petal, right sides together, and match the center marks. Place a pin through the center of each piece and at each end, matching the end marks. With the E piece on top, sew the pieces together along the curved edge, easing to fit as needed. Refer to "Chain Sewing" on page 12 to make the sewing process quicker, if desired. Press the seam allowances toward the E piece. Place a metallic gold-and-green E piece on the opposite side of the F petal, right sides together, and pin in place. Sew and press. The blocks should measure 4½" square. Make a total of 18 curved units with cream petals.

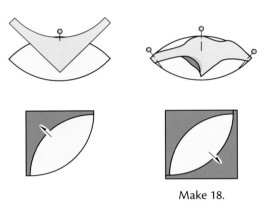

Make 18.

2 Repeat step 1 to make 18 curved units using the medium green F petals and cream E pieces.

Make 18.

Assembling the Quilt Top

1 Arrange the blocks in six horizontal rows of six blocks each, alternating the blocks in each row and from row to row. Rotate every other block 90° so that the petals form diagonal lines across the quilt as shown in the diagram following step 3.

2 Sew the blocks in each row together. Press the seam allowances open.

3 Sew the rows together. Press the seam allowances open. Press the entire quilt center. The quilt center should measure 24½" x 24½".

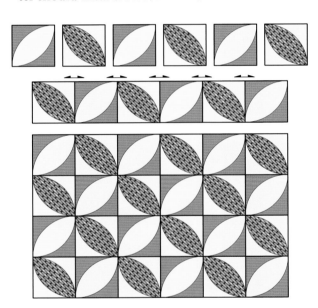

Adding the Borders

1 Sew the 1"-wide green solid strips together end to end to make one long strip.

2 Referring to "Borders" on page 13, measure, cut, and sew the green inner-border strips and then the 5¼"-wide gold-and-green outer-border strips to the quilt top. Press all seam allowances away from the center. Press the entire quilt top.

Finishing the Quilt

Refer to "Quiltmaking Basics" on page 11 as needed to complete the following steps.

1 Layer the quilt top with the batting and backing. Baste the layers together.

2 Hand or machine quilt as desired.

3 Square up the quilt sandwich if needed.

4 Prepare the metallic gold-and-green binding and sew it to the quilt. Add a hanging sleeve, if desired.

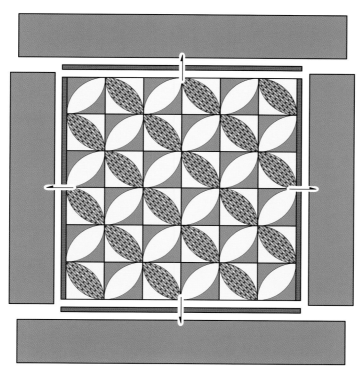

Quilt assembly

Melon Patch

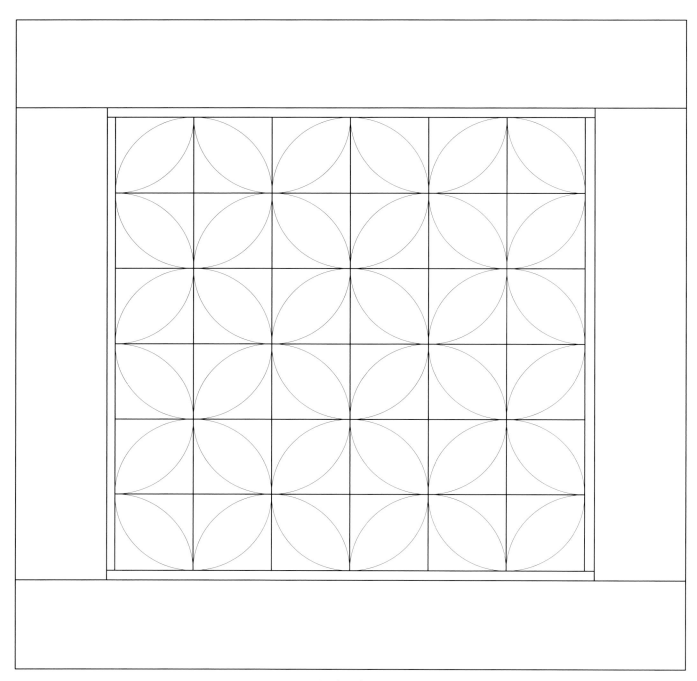

Design sheet

Radiance

Finished Quilt: 35" x 35" • Finished Block: 4" x 4"

Designed and pieced by Tammy Kelly. Machine quilted by Linda DeVries.

Swirls of metallic gold radiate against the fuchsia and purple fabrics in this small but vibrant wall hanging or table centerpiece. The original Spring Beauty block was the inspiration for this artistic quilt.

 ## Fabric-Selection Tips

The two coordinating fuchsia prints take the credit for drawing me to this design. To make interesting petals, I paired a medium purple fabric with a rippled-water appearance to the slightly striped fuchsia-and-purple print. To create contrast and allow the petals to stand out, I matched a dark purple metallic print with the light pink background. A narrow dark purple batik was selected for the inner border that outlines the quilt center. The outer border is a myriad of metallic swirls on a fuchsia-and-purple print.

Materials

All yardages are based on 42" wide fabric.

¾ yard of striped fuchsia-and-purple print for blocks and binding

⅔ yard of dark fuchsia-and-purple swirled print for outer border

⅝ yard of dark purple print for blocks

⅝ yard of light pink solid for blocks

½ yard of medium purple print for blocks

⅛ yard of dark purple batik for inner border

1⅓ yards of fabric for backing

41" x 41" piece of batting

Cutting

All measurements include ¼"-wide seam allowances.

From the dark purple print, cut:
3 strips, 5½" x 42"; crosscut into 18 squares, 5½" x 5½". Cut each square once diagonally to yield 36 half-square triangles.

From the light pink solid, cut:
3 strips, 5½" x 42"; crosscut into 18 squares, 5½" x 5½". Cut each square once diagonally to yield 36 half-square triangles.

From the striped fuchsia-and-purple print, cut:
3 strips, 3¾" x 42"

4 strips, 2½" x 42"

From the medium purple print, cut:
3 strips, 3¾" x 42"

From the dark purple batik, cut:

3 strips, 1" x 42"

From the dark fuchsia-and-purple swirled print, cut:

4 strips, 5¼" x 42"

Making the Blocks

The patterns for templates E and F appear on page 88. For detailed instructions, refer to "Using Curved Templates" on page 8.

1 Sew each dark purple triangle to a light pink triangle to make a half-square-triangle unit. Refer to "Chain Sewing" on page 12 to make the sewing process quicker, if desired. Press the seam allowances open. Make a total of 36 units.

Make 36.

2 Place template E on top of each step 1 unit so that the line on the template is along the seam line and the straight edges of the template are even with the raw edges of the unit. Cut along the curved edge to make 36 E pieces. Repeat by placing the template on the opposite corner of the unit as shown, and cut out along the curved edge to make 36 reverse E pieces. Discard the cutaway pieces, or set them aside for a future project.

Cut 36 E pieces and
36 reversed E pieces.

3 Sew each 3¾" fuchsia-and-purple strip to a medium purple strip as shown to make a strip set. Press the seam allowances open. Make three strip sets.

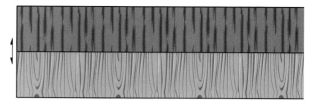

Make 3 strip sets.

4 Place template F on the right side of a strip set so that the line on the template is along the seam line as shown. Cut out a total of 36 F pieces.

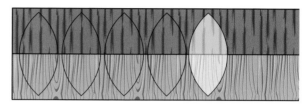

Cut 36 F pieces.

5 To make the pieced curved units, place an E piece from step 2 on top of an F petal from step 4, right sides together, and match the center marks. Place a pin through the center of each piece and at each end, matching the end marks. With the E piece on top, sew the pieces together along the curved edge, easing to fit as needed. Refer to "Chain Sewing" to make the sewing process quicker, if desired. Press the seam allowances toward the E piece. Place a reverse E piece on the opposite side of the petal, right sides together, and pin in place. Sew and press. The blocks should measure 4½" square. Make 36 blocks.

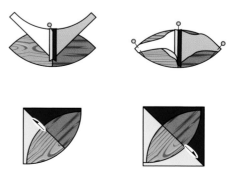

Make 36.

Assembling the Quilt Top

1 Arrange the blocks in six horizontal rows of six blocks each. Rotate every other block 90° so that the fuchsia and purple pieces meet in the center as shown in the diagram following step 3.

2 Sew the blocks in each row together. Press the seam allowances open.

3 Sew the rows together. Press the seam allowances open. Press the entire quilt center. The quilt center should measure 24½" x 24½".

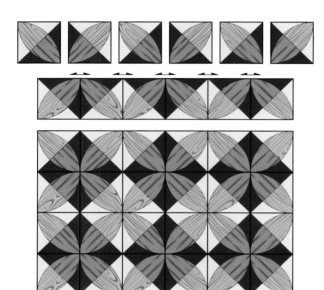

Adding the Borders

1 Sew the 1"-wide dark purple batik strips together end to end to make one long strip.

2 Referring to "Borders" on page 13, measure, cut, and sew the dark purple inner-border strips and

then the 5¼"-wide swirled print outer-border strips to the quilt top. Press all seam allowances away from the center. Press the entire quilt top.

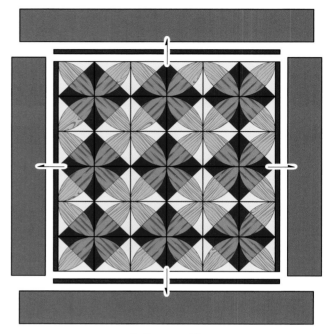

Quilt assembly

Finishing the Quilt

Refer to "Quiltmaking Basics" on page 11 as needed to complete the following steps.

1 Layer the quilt top with the batting and backing. Baste the layers together.

2 Hand or machine quilt as desired.

3 Square up the quilt sandwich if needed.

4 Prepare the striped fuchsia-and-purple binding and sew it to the quilt. Add a hanging sleeve, if desired.

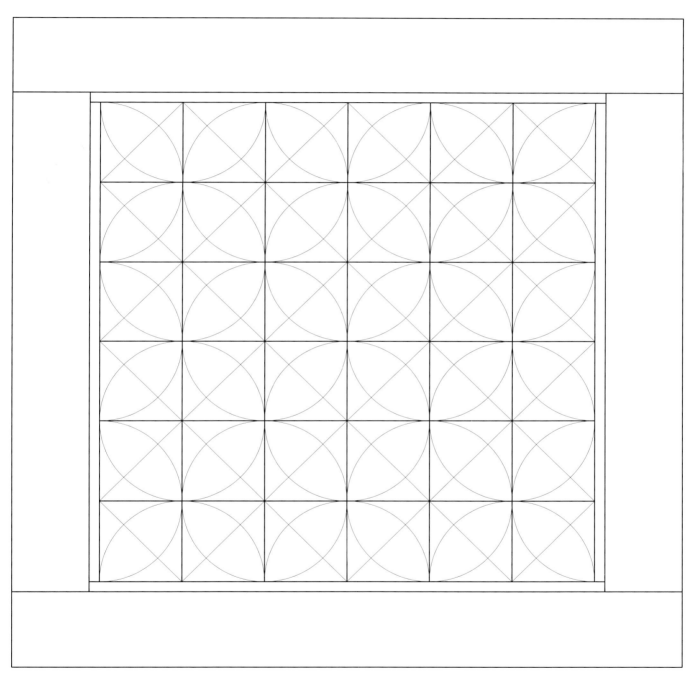

Design sheet

Subtle Shades

Finished Quilt: 35" x 35" ● **Block Size: 4" x 4"**

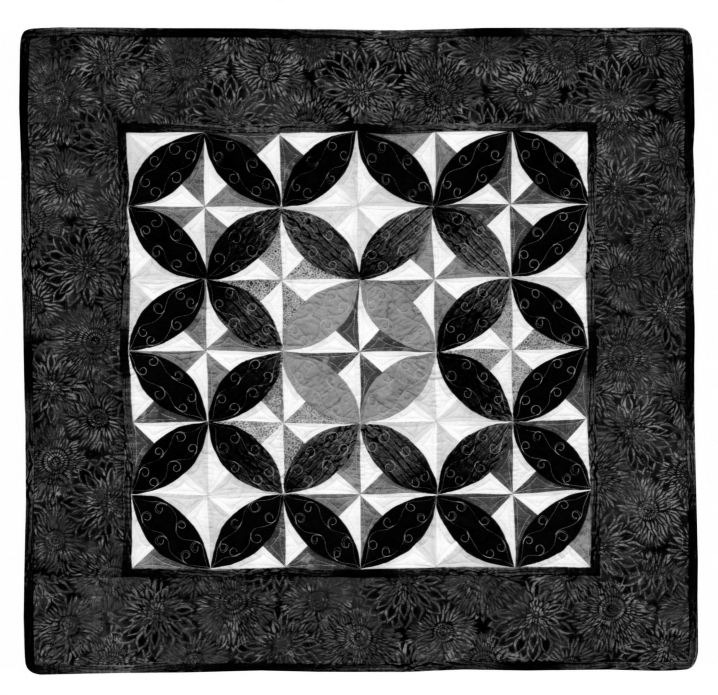

Designed and pieced by Tammy Kelly. Machine quilted by Linda DeVries.

Shades of blended blue and fuchsia fabrics contrast nicely in this stimulating project. Grist Mill is the traditional block name for this unique design.

Fabric-Selection Tips

I was drawn to the outstanding blue-and-fuchsia chrysanthemum batik, which I envisioned as a dynamic outer border. I carefully selected light, medium, and dark blue fabrics for the petals and specifically placed them so the lightest blue is in the center of the quilt. I chose varying shades of four pink fabrics for the background to create curved pinwheels that would add interest, yet not compete with the petals. They are joined with a white background fabric to develop contrast. The blue fabric with the subtle stripe works particularly well for the inner border and binding.

Cutting Suggestion

When cutting the pieces with template F, refer to the diagram on page 51 to make the best use of the fabric.

Materials

All yardages are based on 42"-wide fabric.

⅞ yard of white fabric for blocks

⅔ yard of fuchsia-and-blue large-scale batik for outer border

⅝ yard of medium blue fabric for blocks, inner border, and binding

½ yard of dark blue solid batik for blocks

⅜ yard *each* of light pink, medium pink, and dark pink solid batiks for blocks

¼ yard of medium pink printed batik for blocks

⅛ yard of light blue solid batik for blocks

1⅓ yards of fabric for backing

41" x 41" piece of batting

Cutting

All measurements include ¼"-wide seam allowances. The pattern for template F appears on page 88. For detailed instructions, refer to "Using Curved Templates" on page 8.

From the medium blue fabric, cut:

2 strips, 3" x 42"; cut 12 pieces with template F

4 strips, 2½" x 42"

3 strips, 1" x 42"

From the dark blue solid batik, cut:

4 strips, 3" x 42"; cut 20 pieces with template F

From the light blue solid batik, cut:

1 strip, 3" x 27"; cut 4 pieces with template F

From the white fabric, cut:

5 strips, 5" x 42"; crosscut into 36 squares, 5" x 5".
Cut each square once diagonally to yield 72 half-
square triangles.

**From *each* of the light pink, medium pink, and
dark pink solid batiks, cut:**

2 strips, 5" x 42"; crosscut into 10 squares (30 total),
5" x 5". Cut each square once diagonally to yield
60 half-square triangles.

From the medium pink printed batik, cut:

1 strip, 5" x 42"; crosscut into 6 squares, 5" x 5".
Cut each square once diagonally to yield 12 half-
square triangles.

From the fuchsia-and-blue large-scale batik, cut:

4 strips, 5¼" x 42"

Making the Blocks

*The pattern for template E appears on page 88. For
detailed instructions, refer to "Using Curved Templates"
on page 8.*

1 Sew each white triangle to a pink batik triangle as
shown to make half-square-triangle units. Refer
to "Chain Sewing" on page 12 to make the sewing
process quicker, if desired. Press the seam allowances open. Make a total of 72 units.

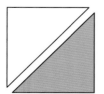

Make 72.

2 Place template E on top of each step 1 unit so that
the line on the template is along the seam line and
the straight edges of the template are even with
the raw edges of the unit. Cut along the curved
edge to make a total of 72 E pieces. Discard the
cutaway leftover pieces or set them aside for a
future project. Note: Each half-square-triangle
unit yields only one of piece E. You do not need a
reverse E piece for this project.

Cut 72.

3 Use a design wall to arrange the light blue F petals,
rotating the petals 90° to form a circle as shown in
the diagram following step 4. Place the medium
blue F petals around the center, and then the dark
blue petals around the outside, again rotating
the petals as shown. Place the pink-and-white E
pieces so that four matching pieces are in the center of each petal arrangement. Place the remaining
pink-and-white pieces around the outside of the
dark blue petals as shown. Once you are pleased
with the arrangement, label all the blocks so that
you'll know where to place them after sewing and
pressing.

4 To make the curved units, place an E piece on
top of a blue F petal, right sides together, and
match the center marks. Place a pin through the
center of each piece and at each end, matching
the end marks. With the E piece on top, sew the
pieces together along the curved edge, easing to fit
as needed. Refer to "Chain Sewing" to make the
sewing process quicker, if desired. Press the seam
allowances toward the E piece. Place an E piece on

the opposite side of the petal, right sides together, and pin in place. Sew and press. The blocks should measure 4½" square. Make 36 blocks.

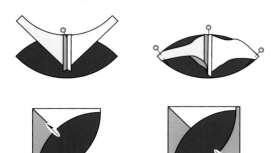

Make 36.

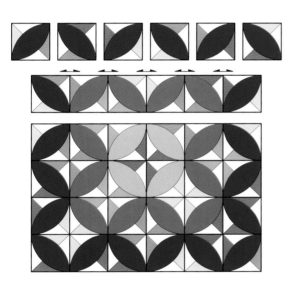

Assembling the Quilt Top

1 Return the completed blocks to your design wall and carefully examine the layout to make sure that each block is placed correctly.

2 Sew the blocks in each row together. Press the seam allowances open.

3 Sew the rows together. Press the seam allowances open. Press the entire quilt center. The quilt center should measure 24½" x 24½".

Adding the Borders

1 Sew the 1"-wide medium blue strips together end to end to make one long strip.

2 Referring to "Borders" on page 13, measure, cut, and sew the medium blue inner-border strips and then the 5¼"-wide fuchsia-and-blue outer-border strips to the quilt top. Press all seam allowances away from the center. Press the entire quilt top.

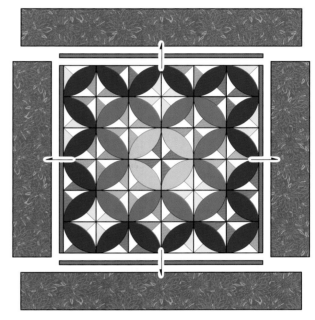

Quilt assembly

Finishing the Quilt

Refer to "Quiltmaking Basics" on page 11 as needed to complete the following steps.

1 Layer the quilt top with the batting and backing. Baste the layers together.

2 Hand or machine quilt as desired.

3 Square up the quilt sandwich if needed.

4 Prepare the medium blue binding and sew it to the quilt. Add a hanging sleeve, if desired.

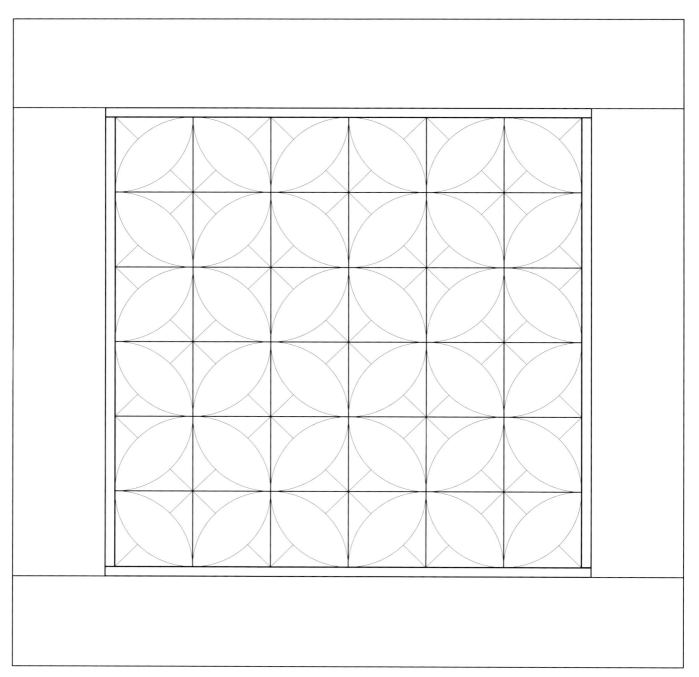

Design sheet

Quiltastic

Finished Quilt: 87½" x 108¾" • **Finished Block: 7" x 7"**

Designed and pieced by Tammy Kelly. Machine quilted by Linda DeVries.

Black contrasts well with the multicolored batiks in this fantastic queen-size quilt with pieced borders. The block is commonly known as Robbing Peter to Pay Paul, and the quilt center can be adapted to any size.

Materials

All yardages are based on 42"-wide fabric.

4¼ yards of black batik for blocks

3¼ yards of dark pink batik for first, fifth, seventh, and Nine Patch borders

2½ yards of light pink batik for third border and binding

⅔ yard of medium purple batik for second and fourth borders

⅓ yard *each* of 39 assorted pink, purple, blue, and green batiks for blocks and Nine Patch border (9 or 10 of each color)

8⅔ yards of fabric for backing

93" x 115" piece of batting

 ## Fabric-Selection Tips

Pink, orange, blue, purple, and green batiks in light, medium, and dark values were my palette. Combined with the black batik, all of those bright fabrics create a pleasing contrast. I wanted to limit the number of curved piecing blocks in the quilt center, so I chose to add a number of borders in varying widths. The dark pink first border frames the quilt center, and the final border in the same fabric contrasts well with the small Nine Patch blocks and the light pink binding. The wide light pink border stands alone between narrow bands of lovely mottled purple. All of these choices allow the eye to be drawn to the quilt center as well as to the pieced border.

Cutting Suggestions

When cutting the pieces with templates G and H, refer to the diagrams below to make the best use of the fabric.

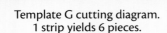

Template G cutting diagram.
1 strip yields 6 pieces.

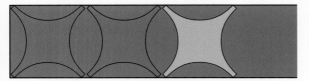

Template H cutting diagram.
1 strip yields 5 pieces.

 ## Yardages for a Full-Size Quilt

To make a full-size (73½" x 94½") quilt, follow the directions on pages 67–69 to make the quilt center, but then add only the first three rounds of borders.

⅝ yard of dark pink batik for first border

⅜ yard of medium purple batik for second border

1⅝ yards of light pink batik for third border

¾ yard of fabric for binding

6⅞ yards of fabric for backing

80" x 101" piece of batting

Cutting

All measurements include ¼"-wide seam allowances. The patterns for templates G and H appear on pages 88 and 89. For detailed instructions, refer to "Using Curved Templates" on page 8.

From the black batik, cut:

30 strips, 2¼" x 42"; cut 176 pieces with template G

9 strips, 8" x 42"; cut 44 pieces with template H

From *each* of 9 of the assorted pink, purple, blue, and green batiks, cut:*

1 strip, 8" x 42" (9 total); cut 44 pieces with template H

From *each* of 30 of the assorted pink, purple, blue, and green batiks, cut:*

1 strip, 2¼" x 42" (30 total); cut 176 pieces with template G

From the remainder of *each* of 27 of the assorted pink, blue, and green batiks, cut:*

2 strips, 1½" x 42" (54 total)

From the dark pink batik, cut:

17 strips, 3½" x 42"; crosscut into 180 squares, 3½" x 3½"

7 strips, 2¼" x 42"

14 strips, 1½" x 42"

5 strips, 1⅝" x 42"

From the medium purple batik, cut:

17 strips, 1¼" x 42"

From the light pink batik, cut:

8 strips, 6½" x 42"

11 strips, 2½" x 42"

*Be sure to cut the 39 assorted pink, blue, purple, and green batiks in the order listed to achieve the desired number of strips.

Making the Blocks

1 Place any G piece (except black) on top of a black H piece, right sides together, and match the center marks. Place a pin through the center of each piece and at each end, matching the end marks. With the G piece on top, sew the pieces together along the curved edge. Sew slowly at first, removing the pins as you come to them and easing to fit as needed. Press the seam allowances toward the G piece. Repeat to sew a G piece of a different color to the opposite side, and then to each remaining side. The block should measure 7½" square. Make a total of 44 blocks.

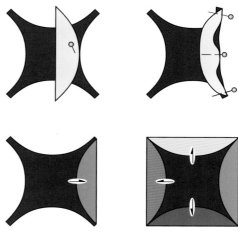

Make 44.

2 Repeat step 1, sewing a pink, purple, blue, or green H piece and four black G pieces together as shown. Make 44 blocks.

Make 44.

Assembling the Quilt Top

1 Lay out the blocks in 11 horizontal rows of eight blocks each. Alternate the blocks in each row and from row to row as shown in the diagram following step 3.

2 Sew the blocks in each row together. Press the seam allowances open.

3 Sew the rows together. Press the seam allowances open. Press the entire quilt center. The quilt center should measure 56½" x 77½".

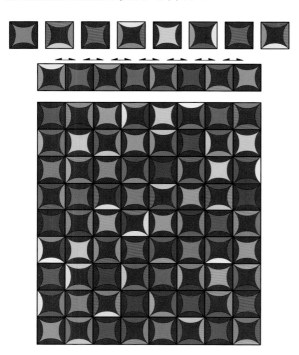

Making the Nine Patch Border

1 To make the Nine Patch blocks, sew three 1½" x 42" assorted pink strips together along the long edges as shown to make strip set A. Repeat using different pink strips to make strip sets B and C. Make 2 of each strip set and press the seam allowances as shown. The strip sets should measure 3½" wide. Crosscut each strip set into 29 segments, 1½" wide.

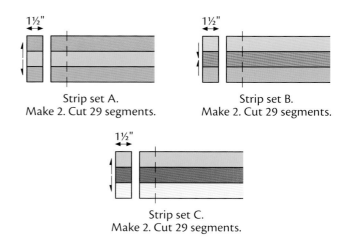

Strip set A.
Make 2. Cut 29 segments.

Strip set B.
Make 2. Cut 29 segments.

Strip set C.
Make 2. Cut 29 segments.

2 Arrange one segment each from strip sets A, B, and C as shown. Sew the segments together. Press the seam allowances away from the center segment to complete a Nine Patch block. The block should measure 3½" square. Make 29 pink blocks.

Make 29.

3 Repeat steps 1 and 2 using the 1½" x 42" blue strips. Make 28 blue blocks.

Make 28.

4 Repeat steps 1 and 2 using the 1½" x 42" green strips. Make 29 green blocks.

Make 29.

5 Sew a pink, blue, or green Nine Patch block between two 3½" dark pink squares as shown. Refer to "Chain Sewing" on page 12 to make the sewing process quicker, if desired. Press seam allowances toward the dark pink squares. Make 86 border units. (You'll have eight dark pink squares left over to use in steps 6 and 7.)

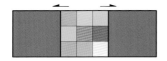

Make 86.

6 To make a side border, sew 23 border units from step 5 together, alternating the green, pink, and blue Nine Patch blocks as shown in the photo on page 65. Sew a 3½" dark pink square to the top and bottom of the pieced strip as shown. Press the seam allowances toward the dark pink squares. Trim ¼" from the crossed seams on all sides as shown. Discard the remaining dark pink fabric or set it aside for a future project. The Nine Patch border strip should measure 4¾" x 98¼". Make two side border strips.

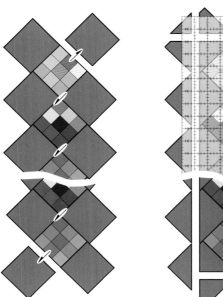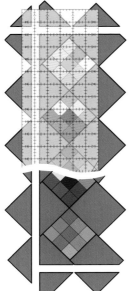

7 Repeat step 6, using 20 border units from step 5 to make the top border strip and then the bottom border strip. The border strips should measure 4¾" x 85½".

Adding the Borders

For detailed instructions, refer to "Borders" on page 13.

1 Sew the 2¼"-wide dark pink strips together end to end to make one long strip. Measure, cut, and sew the dark pink first border to the quilt top. Press the seam allowances toward the border strips. The quilt top should measure 60" x 81".

2 Using eight of the 1¼"-wide medium purple strips, repeat step 1 to measure, cut, and sew the second border to the quilt top. The quilt top should measure 61½" x 82½".

3 Using the 6½"-wide light pink strips, repeat step 1 to measure, cut, and sew the third border to the quilt top. The quilt top should measure 73½" x 94½".

4 Using the remaining 1¼"-wide medium purple strips, repeat step 1 to measure, cut, and sew the fourth border to the quilt top. The quilt top should measure 75" x 96".

5 To add the fifth border, sew the 1⅝"-wide dark pink strips end to end to make one long strip. Measure the quilt from top to bottom and cut two strips from the long strip to fit that measurement. Sew the strips to the side edges of the quilt top; press.

6 Sew four of the 1½"-wide dark pink strips end to end to make one long strip. Measure the quilt from side to side, including the just-added borders, and cut two strips from the long strip to that measurement. Sew the strips to the top and bottom edges of the quilt top; press. The quilt top should measure 77" x 98¼".

7 Pin-mark the center of the quilt sides. Mark the center of each Nine Patch side border strip. With right sides together, match the centers and ends of the quilt and border strips; pin along the sides, easing to fit as needed. Sew the borders in place. Press seam allowances toward the center of the quilt top.

8 Repeat step 7 to sew the top and bottom Nine Patch border strips to the quilt top.

9 Using the remaining 1½"-wide dark pink strips, repeat step 1 to measure, cut, and sew the strips to the quilt top. Press the seam allowances away from the center. Press the entire quilt top.

Finishing the Quilt

Refer to "Quiltmaking Basics" on page 11 as needed to complete the following steps.

1 Layer the quilt top with the batting and backing. Baste the layers together.

2 Hand or machine quilt as desired.

3 Square up the quilt sandwich if needed.

4 Prepare the light pink binding and sew it to the quilt. Add a hanging sleeve, if desired.

Quilt assembly

Square-in-a-Square Units

1 Sew a 2½" light blue triangle to one side of each 2¾" dark purple square, right sides together. Press the seam allowances toward the triangle.

2 Sew a light blue triangle to the three remaining sides of each dark purple square; press. The square-in-a-square unit should measure 3¾" square. Make four units.

Make 4.

Assembling the Block

1 To make the Scrap Blossoms block, place a square-in-a-square unit on the upper-left corner of one unit B rectangle as shown, right sides together. Sew the pieces together, stopping at the center of the square. Finger-press the seam allowance away from the center unit. Make four.

Stop stitching.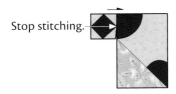

2 Sew one unit A rectangle to the top edge of each unit from step 1 as shown; finger-press. Make four.

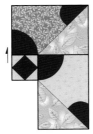

3 Sew one unit B rectangle to the left side of each unit from step 2; finger-press. Then sew one unit A rectangle along the bottom edge of each unit; finger-press. Sew the remaining portion of the seam of the first unit B rectangle to the center unit to complete the block. Make a total of four blocks, making sure each block is sewn together in the same order.

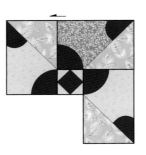 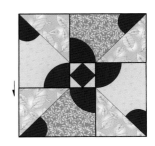

Make 4.

Assembling the Quilt Top

1 Lay out the blocks in two horizontal rows of two blocks each.

2 Sew the blocks in each row together. Press the seam allowances in alternate directions from row to row.

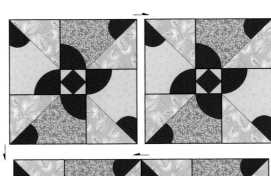

3 Sew the rows together. Press the seam allowances in one direction. Press the entire quilt center. The quilt center should measure 32½" square.

4 Referring to "Borders" on page 13, measure, cut, and sew the 2¼"-wide purple-and-white inner-border strips to the quilt top, and then the 2¾"-wide dark purple outer-border strips. Press all seam allowances away from the center. Press the entire quilt top.

Finishing the Quilt

Refer to "Quiltmaking Basics" on page 11 as needed to complete the following steps.

1 Layer the quilt top with the batting and backing. Baste the layers together.

2 Hand or machine quilt as desired.

3 Square up the quilt sandwich if needed.

4 Prepare the purple-and-white print binding and sew it to the quilt. Add a hanging sleeve, if desired.

Quilt assembly

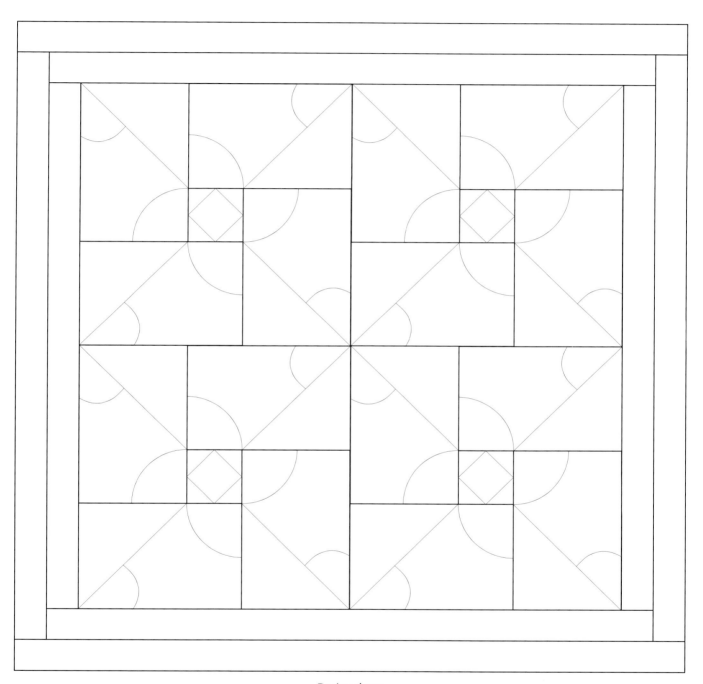

Design sheet

Blazing Star

Finished Quilt: 43" x 62½" • **Block Size: 16" x 16"**

Designed and pieced by Tammy Kelly. Machine quilted by Linda DeVries.

Fabric-Selection Tips

Schemes of 10 analogous colors ranging from spring green to red-tinged violet are included in this design. By choosing fabrics that are all batiks, I created a colorwash effect. The Blazing Star blocks contain light blue and light green background fabrics, which contrast well against the reddish violet and dark bluish violet petals in each star. Reddish violet circles light up the center of each Blazing Star. The varied medium and dark sashing strips and light squares frame the blocks, eliminating the need for additional borders.

Cutting Suggestions

When cutting the pieces with templates L, M, N, and O, refer to the diagrams below to make the best use of the fabric.

Template L cutting diagram.
1 strip yields 8 pieces.

Template M cutting diagram.
1 strip yields 5 pieces.

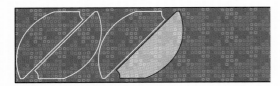

Template N cutting diagram.
1 strip yields 8 pieces.

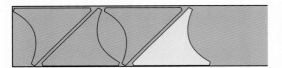

Template O cutting diagram.
1 strip yields 6 pieces.

Materials

All yardages are based on 42"-wide fabric.

⅞ yard of light blue batik for blocks

⅔ yard of dark purple batik for sashing

⅝ yard of light green batik for blocks

⅝ yard of light reddish violet batik for appliqué circles and binding

⅝ yard *each* of 2 assorted dark blue batiks for blocks

½ yard *each* of 3 assorted dark reddish violet batiks for blocks

⅓ yard *each* of 3 assorted medium blue-and-purple batiks for sashing

⅓ yard of light purple batik for sashing squares

3 yards of fabric for backing

49" x 69" piece of batting

Freezer paper

Cutting

All measurements include ¼"-wide seam allowances. The patterns for templates L, M, N, and O appear on pages 92–94. For detailed instructions, refer to "Using Curved Templates" on page 8.

From the light green batik, cut:
3 strips, 5¾" x 42"; cut 24 pieces with template L

From the light blue batik, cut:
4 strips, 6½" x 42"; cut 24 pieces with template O

From *each* of the 2 assorted dark blue batiks, cut:
2 strips, 3¾" x 42" (4 total); cut a total of 14 pieces with template M

1 strip, 8" x 42" (2 total); cut a total of 10 pieces with template N

From *each* of the 3 assorted dark reddish violet batiks, cut:

1 strip, 3¾" x 42" (3 total); cut a total of 10 pieces with template M

1 strip, 8" x 42" (3 total); cut a total of 14 pieces with template N

From the dark purple batik, cut:

5 strips, 4" x 42"; crosscut into 10 pieces, 4" x 16½"

From the 3 assorted medium blue-and-purple batiks, cut a *total* of:

7 pieces, 4" x 16½"

From the light purple batik, cut:

2 strips, 4" x 42"; crosscut into 12 squares, 4" x 4"

From the light reddish violet batik, cut:

6 strips, 2½" x 42"

Making the Blocks

This quilt consists of three blocks. Block A has short reddish violet petals and long dark blue petals. Block B has short dark blue petals and long reddish violet petals. Block C has a combination of both short and long reddish violet petals and dark blue petals.

Block A

1 Place a reddish violet M piece on top of a light blue O piece, right sides together, and match the center marks. Place a pin through the center of each piece and at each end, matching the end marks. With the M piece on top, sew the pieces together along the curved edge. Sew slowly at first, removing the pins as you come to them and easing to fit as needed. Press the seam allowances

toward the O piece. Make 10 units. (Set aside two matching units for block C.)

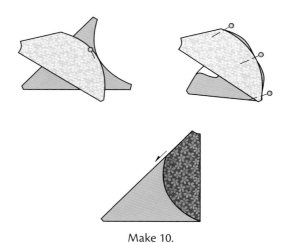

Make 10.

2 Place a dark blue N piece on top of a light green L piece, right sides together, and match the center marks. Place a pin through the center of each piece and at each end, matching the end marks. With the N piece on top, sew the pieces together along the curved edge. Sew slowly at first, removing the pins as you come to them and easing to fit as needed. Press the seam allowances toward the L piece. Make 10 units. (Set aside two matching units for block C.)

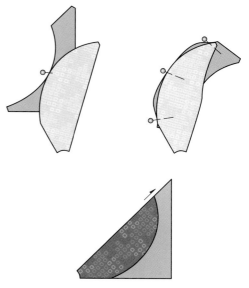

Make 10.

3 Using four matching light blue units from step 1 and four matching light green units from step 2, sew a blue unit to each green unit as shown. Press the seam allowances toward the green unit. The units should now measure 8½" square. Make four matching units.

4 Repeat step 3 to sew the remaining light blue units and light green units together to make four matching units; press. The units should now measure 8½" square.

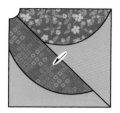
Make 4.

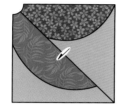
Make 4.

5 Arrange two units from step 3 and two units from step 4 as shown. Sew the units in rows and press the seam allowances to one side. With right sides together, carefully pin and sew the top of the block and the bottom of the block together, leaving a hole in the center. Press the seam allowances to one side. Press the entire block. The block should measure 16½" square. Make two blocks.

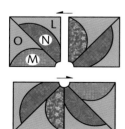
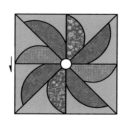
Block A.
Make 2.

Block B

1 Place a dark blue M piece on top of a light blue O piece, right sides together, and match the center marks. Place a pin through the center of each piece and at each end, matching the end marks. With the M piece on top, sew the pieces together along the curved edge. Sew slowly at first, removing the pins as you come to them and easing to fit as needed. Press the seam allowances toward the O piece. Make 14 units. (Set aside two matching units for block C.)

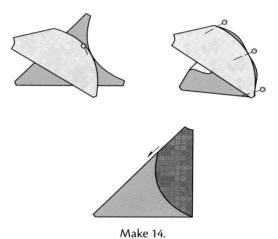
Make 14.

2 Place a reddish violet N piece on top of a light green L piece, right sides together, and match the center marks. Place a pin through the center of each piece and at each end, matching the end marks. With the N piece on top, sew the pieces together along the curved edge. Sew slowly at first, removing the pins as you come to them and

easing to fit as needed. Press the seam allowances toward the L piece. Make 14 units. (Set aside two matching units for block C.)

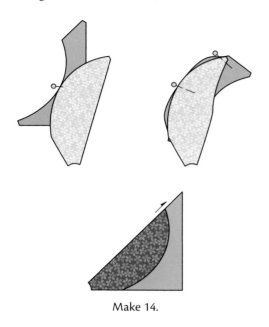

Make 14.

3 Using six matching light blue units from step 1 and six matching light green units from step 2, sew a blue unit to each green unit as shown. Press the seam allowances toward the green unit. The units should now measure 8½" square. Make six matching units.

4 Sew the remaining light blue units and light green units together to make six matching units; press. The units should now measure 8½" square.

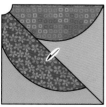

Make 6.   Make 6.

5 Arrange two units from step 3 and two units from step 4 as shown. Sew the units in rows and press the seam allowances to one side. With right sides together, carefully pin and sew the top of the block and the bottom of the block together, leaving a hole in the center. Press the seam allowances to one side. Press the entire block. The block should measure 16½" square. Make three blocks.

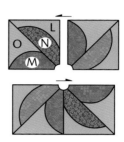
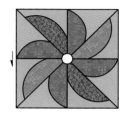

Block B.
Make 3.

Block C

1 Using the units from steps 1 and 2 of "Block A," sew a light blue unit to each light green unit. Press the seam allowances toward the green unit. The units should now measure 8½" square. Make two units.

2 Using the units from steps 1 and 2 of "Block B," sew a light blue unit to each light green unit. Press the seam allowances toward the green unit. The units should now measure 8½" square. Make two units.

3 Arrange the units from steps 1 and 2 as shown. Sew the units in rows and press the seam allowances to one side. With right sides together, carefully pin and sew the top of the block and the bottom of the block together, leaving a hole in

the center. Press the seam allowances to one side. Press the entire block. The block should measure 16½" square.

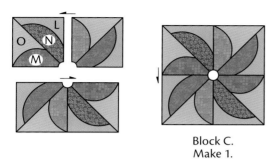

Block C.
Make 1.

Appliqué

1 Using the pattern on page 94, trace six of template P onto freezer paper. Cut out the freezer-paper templates on the traced lines. Using a hot, dry iron, press the shiny side of the freezer paper to the wrong side of the light reddish violet fabric.

2 Trim the fabric around the paper template, leaving ¼" for seam allowance.

3 Use scissors to make small snips around the outside edge of each circle, stopping just before reaching the freezer paper. Press the raw edges to the wrong side, toward the freezer paper, until a circle is formed.

Make 6.

4 Place a fabric circle in the center of each block and pin in place. Using a medium-length blanket stitch and matching thread, stitch along the curved edge of the circle by machine or by hand.

Turn the block to the wrong side and carefully remove the freezer paper. If you need to use scissors to cut the freezer paper, be careful not to cut through the fabric. Repeat to complete six Blazing Star blocks.

Make 6.

Assembling the Quilt Top

1 Referring to the quilt assembly diagram, sew a 4" x 16½" blue-and-purple piece between two blocks. Press the seam allowances toward the sashing strip. Then add a 4" x 16½" dark purple piece to the left and right sides to make a block row. Make three rows.

2 Sew three 4" light purple squares and two 4" x 16½" blue-and-purple pieces together, alternating them as shown in the assembly diagram. Press the seam allowances toward the sashing strips. Make two blue-and-purple sashing rows.

3 Repeat step 2 using three 4" light purple squares and two 4" x 16½" dark purple pieces. Make two dark purple sashing rows.

4 Sew the block rows and sashing rows together as shown in the assembly diagram. Press the seam allowances toward the sashing rows. Press the entire quilt top. The quilt should measure 43" x 62½".

Finishing the Quilt

Refer to "Quiltmaking Basics" on page 11 as needed to complete the following steps.

1. Layer the quilt top with the batting and backing. Baste the layers together.

2. Hand or machine quilt as desired.

3. Square up the quilt sandwich if needed.

4. Prepare the light reddish violet binding and sew it to the quilt. Add a hanging sleeve, if desired.

Quilt assembly

Blazing Star

Design sheet

Template Patterns

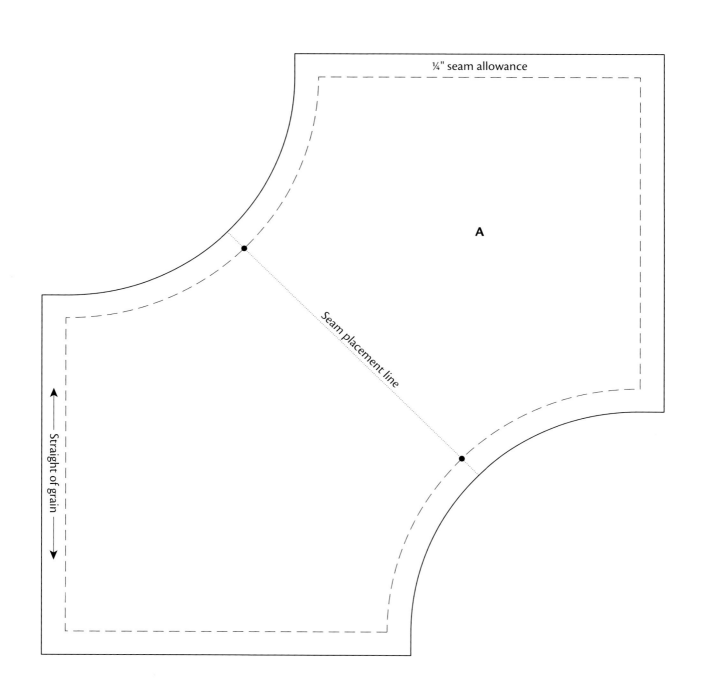

¼" seam allowance

A

Seam placement line

Straight of grain

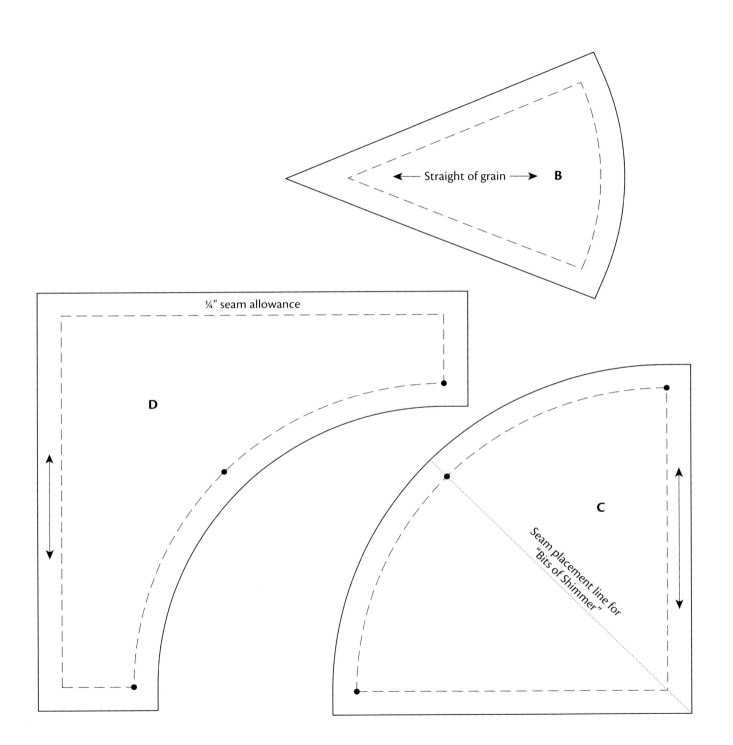

Template Patterns

Straight of grain

B

¼" seam allowance

D

C

Seam placement line for "Bits of Shimmer"

87

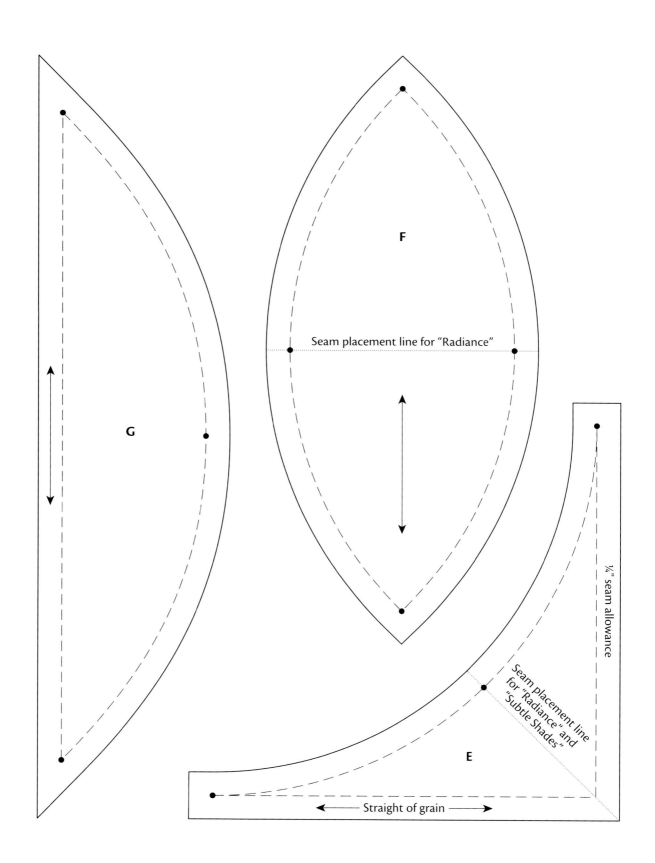

G

F

Seam placement line for "Radiance"

¼" seam allowance

Seam placement line for "Radiance" and "Subtle Shades"

E

Straight of grain

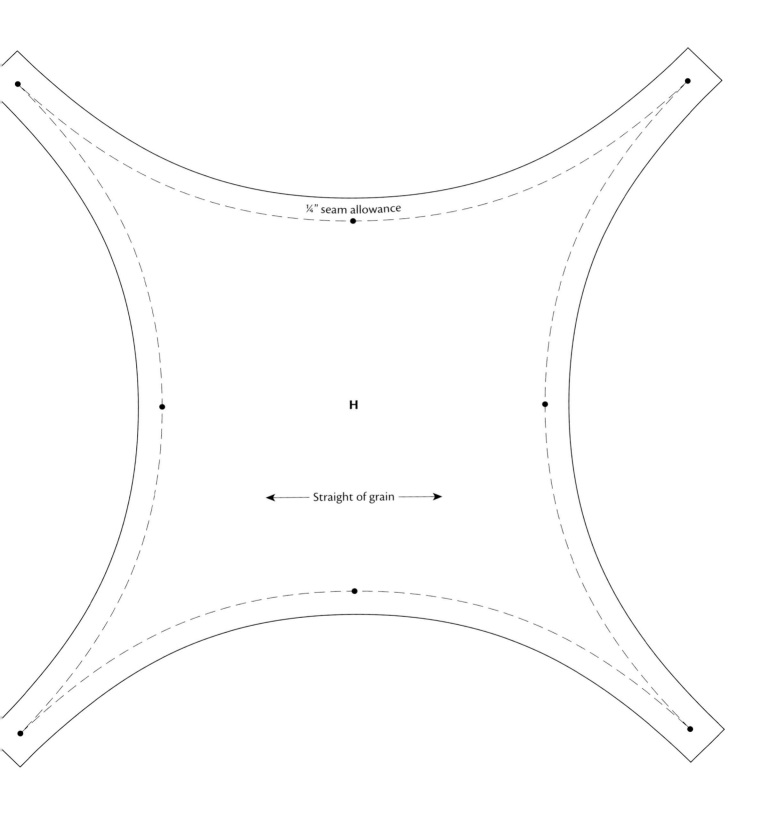

¼" seam allowance

H

Straight of grain

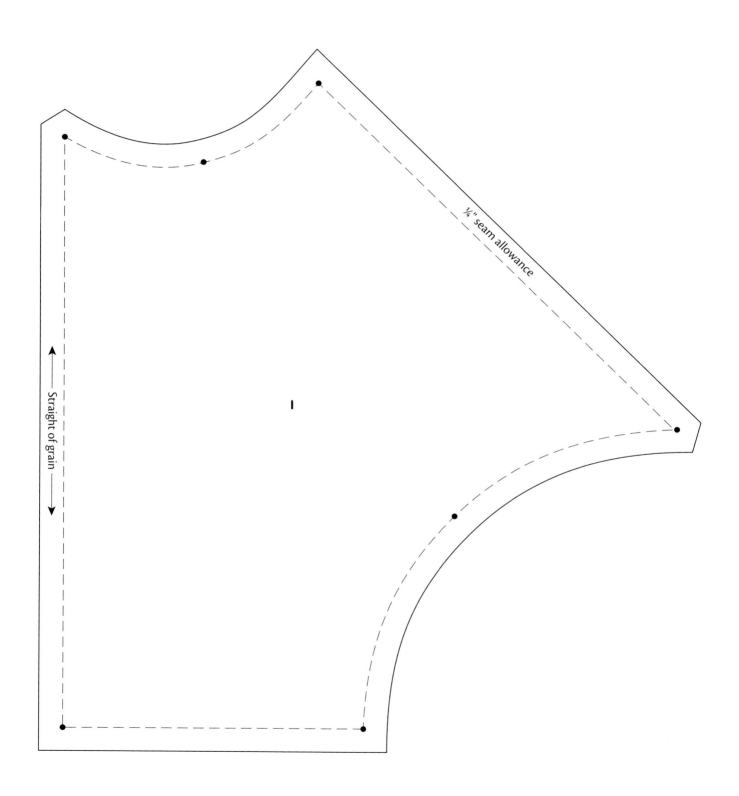

¼" seam allowance

Straight of grain

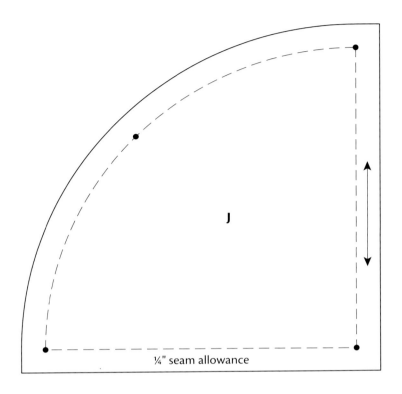

J

¼" seam allowance

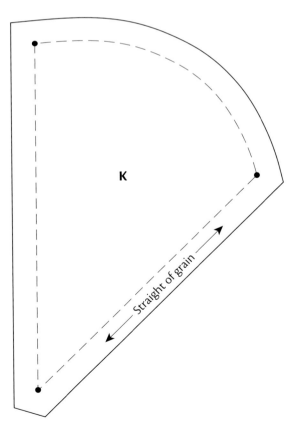

K

Straight of grain

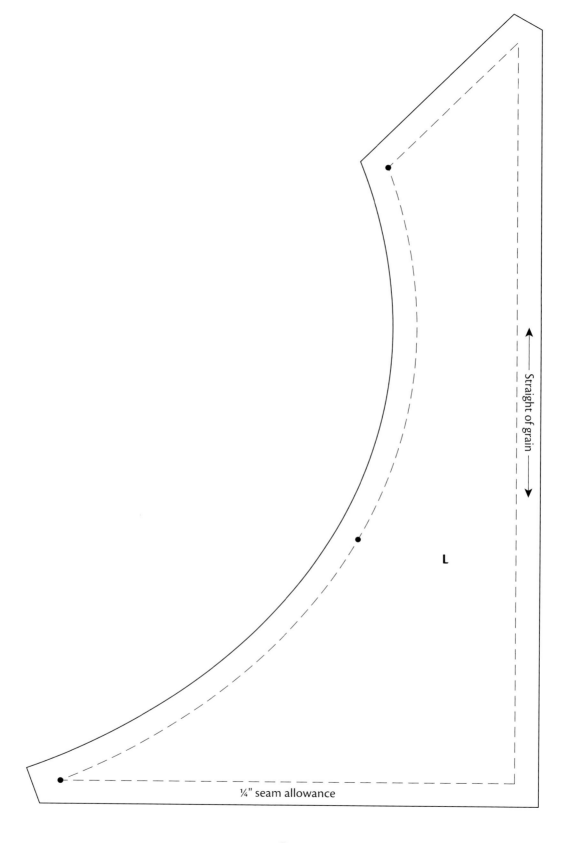

Straight of grain

L

¼" seam allowance

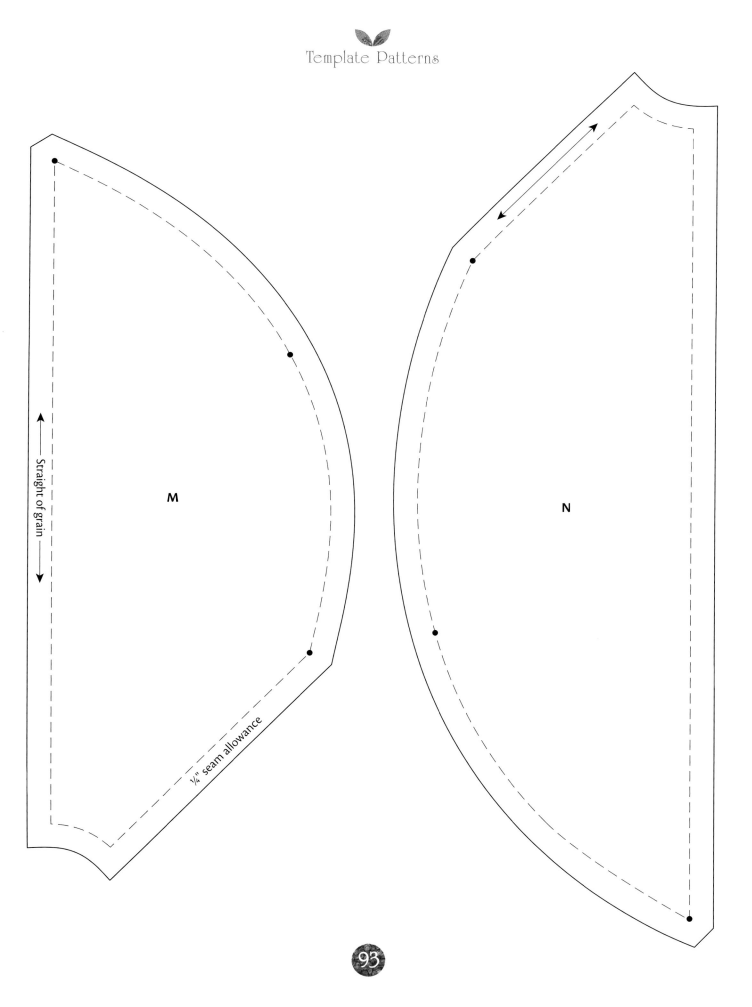

Straight of grain

M

¼" seam allowance

N

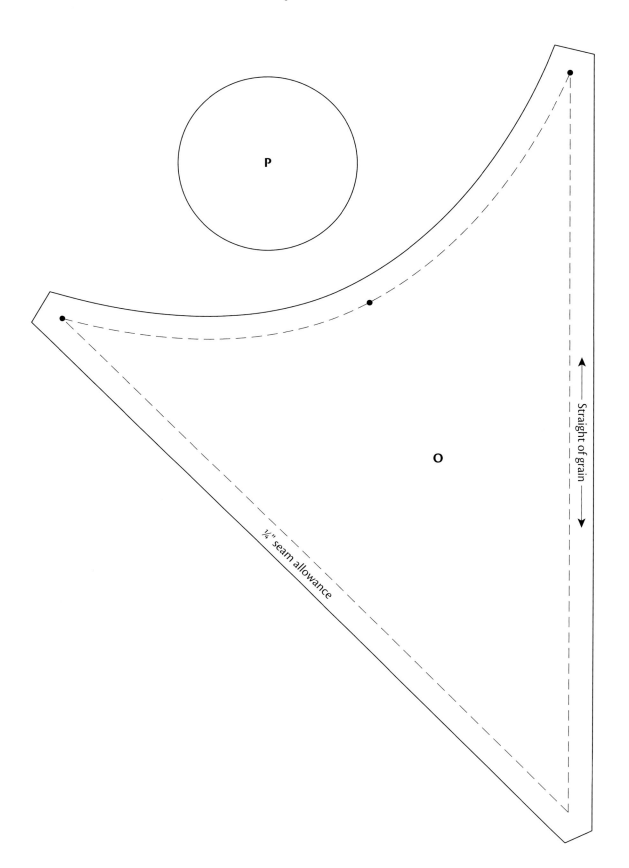

P

O

Straight of grain

¼" seam allowance

Resources

Common Threads
Tammy Kelly
8150 Wendy's Way
Flagstaff, AZ 86004
928-527-0508
tkelly@ourcommonthreads.com
www.ourcommonthreads.com
*All curved piecing templates are available from
Common Threads or your local quilt shop.*

Hoffman California Fabrics
25792 Obrero Dr.
Mission Viejo, CA 92691
949-770-2922
www.hoffmanfabrics.com

Michael Miller Fabrics
118 W. 22nd St.
New York, NY 10011
212-704-0774
www.michaelmillerfabrics.com

OLFA-North America Division
5500 N. Pearl St., Suite 400
Rosemont, IL 60018
847-233-8762
www.olfa.com

Quilt Dance
www.quiltdance.com
*Tag-A-Quilt printed Mylar labels are available
in independent quilt stores.*

About the Author

Tammy Kelly is a quilt designer, teacher, and author. She teaches quilting at regional quilt shops, quilt camps, and her local community college, and it is her desire to someday teach internationally. She draws upon all of her experience as an elementary school teacher when planning and conducting a quilt class. She also encourages her students to be creative with fabric selection and design.

Tammy's favorite quilting topic is COLOR! The fabric "talks" to her and she carefully chooses just the right color combination for each individual quilt. Exploring patterns and color values is her passion. Her favorite quilt is always the next one—the one that is yet to be created. She is inspired by patterns in nature, home decor, and other artists.

Many of her quilts have been published in national quilting magazines and calendars. She also publishes her own pattern line called Common Threads. Tammy is the author of two additional quilting books, including *Snowball Quilts* (Martingale & Company, 2007).

A view of the San Francisco peaks from Tammy's sewing-room studio in Flagstaff, Arizona, also provides inspiration and encourages reflection. Tammy lives with her husband, Dave, and daughter, Lynnae. She feels blessed to have special friends with whom to share her creative endeavors.